DESIGN SIMULATION

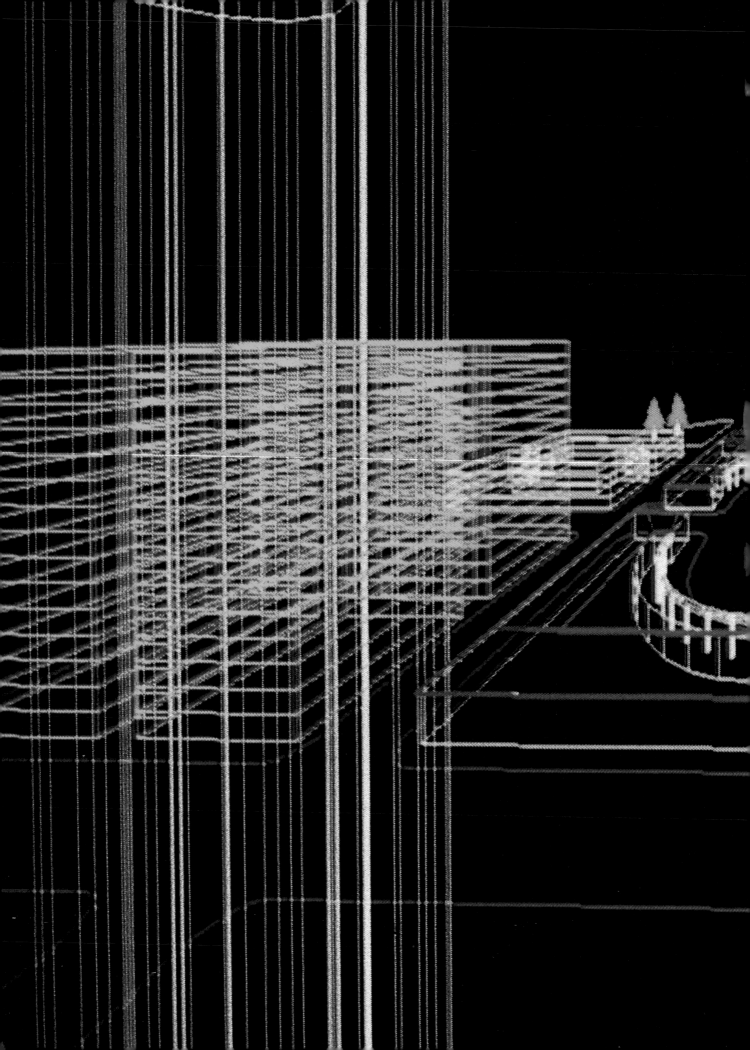

DESIGN SIMULATION

Use Of Photographic
And Electronic
Media In Design
And Presentation

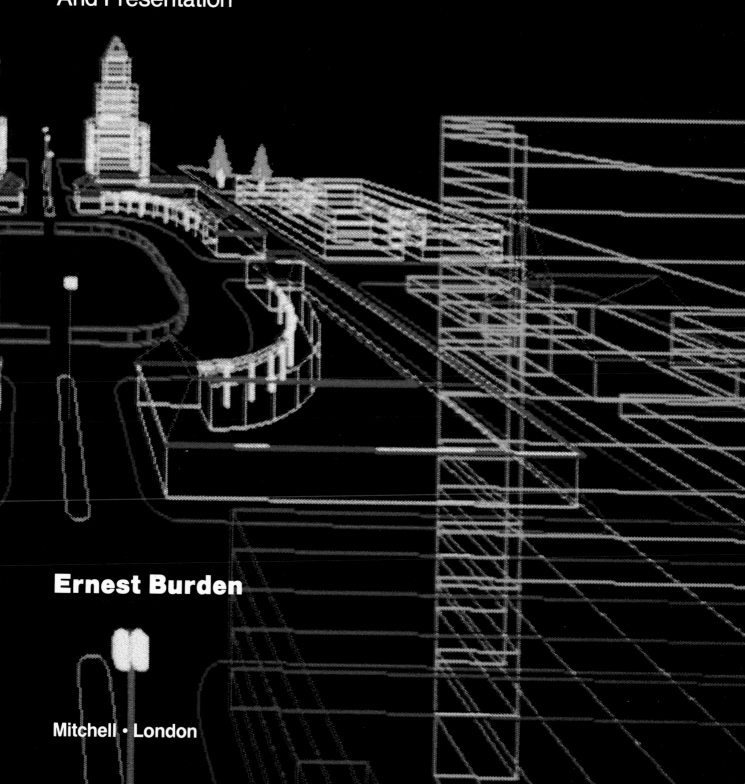

Ernest Burden

Mitchell • London

ACKNOWLEDGMENTS

The simulation of design is, in most cases, an early stage in the life of a project. Design features are often altered as a result of the simulation. This truly demonstrates the value of seeing a replication of the object prior to its construction.

Therefore, I want to thank all the design firms listed in the Design Credits for permission to publish their early design studies and conceptual sketches, and other presentation material.

A special thanks to my friend and colleague Hans—Christian Lischewski for providing the many fine examples of visualization techniques that enhance these pages, and for the introduction to this edition.

This book is the result of a coordinated effort by many people in the printing and publishing industry, and I want to particularly thank senior editor Julia Moore for her insight and assistance in getting this edition published. This book is the culmination of all those efforts, plus many more from other people behind the scenes, whose contributions are also greatly appreciated.

First published in 1988 in Great Britain by
The Mitchell Publishing Company Limited
4 Fitzhardinge Street, London W1H 0AH
A subsidiary of B.T. Batsford Limited
ISBN 0 7134 6095 4

Library of Congress Cataloging-in-Publication Data

Burden, Ernest E., 1934
  Design Simulation.

  Includes index.
  1. Architectural design—Simulation methods.
  2. Architectural design—Data processing. I. Title.
  NA2750.B863 1988   729   88—10
  ISBN 0—8230—1324—3

Copyright © 1985,1988 by Ernest Burden

Book design and layout by Ernest Burden

Manufactured in U.S.A.

First printing, 1988

1 2 3 4 5 6 7 8 9/93 92 91 90 89 88

PREFACE

Design and project simulation involves methods of translating conceptual ideas into visual forms. Although at its root the idea has been the same throughout history, it takes on many forms of expression. These expressions are mainly the result of technological advances in producing imagery, rather than in the ideas themselves. Historically the role of simulation has been instrumental in design exploration and communication.

Today there are many more forms of simulation available to us. Of these, the art of programming is assuming more and more importance. This activity involves identifying elements and activities that will ultimately affect the finished product. It means organizing the elements into a matrix to study the impact that each element will have on the other, and to simulat graphically what the completed space will be like.

The outcome of the program generates the design concepts, which are expressed in design study sketches. When the design becomes more refined and solidified, perspective drawings can be produced. Photography can be used to facilitate the design process. Through composite images or photomontages, photographs of drawings or models can be set into the exact environment and provide a totally realistic simulation of the way the project will look when completed.

Scale models represent the closest simulation to the real thing, since the project is already in a three-dimensional mode and any photograph or visual representation of it will be all the more realistic.

Film and videotape technology can add movement using a scale model, producing one of the most realistic simulations possible, that of traveling through the space.

Computer design and graphics will play a major role in conceptual design, technical design, and design communication. Once a project is defined and its parameters are stored in the computer memory bank, a vast number of alternatives can be generated and viewed dynamically, as though the viewer were moving in and around the building. A computer interface with video makes it possible to record and also to play back these simulations. The technology is presently available to produce such simulations in three-dimensional stereo imagery. Laser and video-disc technology will make it possible to store and retrieve a multitude of images instantaneously. The combination of electronic media available, wherein computers and lasers can generate images that can be portrayed in holographic form, will certainly have a great impact on the way design professionals communicate their design concepts. The purpose of these simulations is to communicate through visual means—a process that's gone on for over 25,000 years.

Ernest Burden

INTRODUCTION: Paperback Edition

In creating design simulations, the architect and designer create stand-ins for reality— the reality being the unbuilt building or buildings, and the stand-ins being the whole range of visualizations from sketches to video photography of models and three-dimensional CADD modeling programs.

Architectural design visualization methods have been an essential part of the architectural design process for at least 2,000 years, and probably much longer. The Egyptians made scale models and concept sketches, two of the simplest visualizations, to communicate their design ideas. Over the centuries, more sophisticated visualizations and simulations have evolved. But the purpose is the same as it always was: to support the design communication process so that everyone involved in the "buying," approval, and building of the project can see what the architect visualized.

Today's architect can use a variety of visualization methods to preview a design and present it to others. Although one of the most popular tools for spontaneous design seems to be the sketch on a restaurant napkin, architects do use other, more sophisticated methods.

During the successive phases of the design process, the complexity of information increases. Visualization of preliminary design studies might only include information about functions, adjacency, areas, and volumes. Later, when most of the design decisions are final and construction documents and specifications are being produced, design visualization in the form of renderings or models might include information about materials, colors, and textures. Each phase will require different methods of visualization because of different degrees of the abstraction and complexity of the space to be displayed. And there are certain experiential conditions- such as space, movement, sound, smell and light- that cannot be simulated with standard visualization methods.

The best way to produce visualization with the utmost reality would be to build the reality at full scale. So far, only Hollywood has produced near-perfect, large-scale "architectural simulations" in the form of science-fiction films, westerns, and historical movies. Because in these film genres nothing actually exists, an artificial environment has to be built. Actors simulate certain activities within a film set. The result of such a simulation is the movie. As a final product, the simulation itself is intended to generate a profit. Therefore, its production is financed by an enourmous budget.

Architectural simulation, on the contrary, is regarded only as a design-supporting method and usually receives a very small fraction of the total budget for a project. As a result, architects and designers have developed architecture-specific simulation methods that are cost-effective. Drawings, models, model photography, video, and now computer applications provide a wide range of affordable methods to preview and explore a new design.

When Design Simulation was conceived, computer-aided design—especially three-dimensional architectural modeling—was in a relatively early stage of development. Since then, both hardware and software have improved and have come down drastically in cost. During the last few years, computer-aided design and drafting has become a cost-saving, interdisciplinary tool, supporting all phases of the design and production process.

Recognizing that to achieve the best results within a realistic architectural budget means mastering a number of different visualization techniques, this book includes traditional methods, such as the building of scale models, rendering, and photography. In many cases, it works best to combine various techniques to achieve optimum effectiveness, and this book gives an overview of the palette of simulation techniques and shows how they have been used and integrated in different projects.

With today's evolving building methods, individual design styles, and fast-paced construction, the need to pre-visualize is becoming increasingly important. New, sophisticated techniques have been developed. Computer graphics are becoming feasible as a presentation and design tool. And although their dominant application is still project-related design visualization, we can observe a trend toward video and holography for marketing and promotion. True three-dimensional displays in the form of stereoscopic CRT displays or "instant" holograms of computer-generated models will be the next step. Such research is currently being done for the space and automotive industries, as well as for a variety of medical applications.

The design workstation of the future will allow the architect to preview and fine tune a design on the CRT screen. Special display and viewing devices are currently under development to generate a realistic walk-through simulation of an architectural space in real-time. The design will be perceived from the inside in true 3-D, without limiting the viewer by an image border, such as a sheet of paper or a monitor surface.

I hope this book, with its overview of traditional and advanced architectural simulation techniques, will be used to support architects in their design work and to stimulate new developments in architectural visualization. If these new techniques are applied appropriately, they will not only make the design process more efficient and clear to everyone involved, but will, it is hoped, result in excellent architectural design.

Hans-Christian Lischewski

1 The Design Process

The elements of the process are examined in terms of programming, methodology, orientation and the design process. Examples from case study projects illustrate these major points and their relationship to describing the elements that influence preliminary design decisions.

2 Drawing Simulation

Traditional methods of depicting buildings and their environments are illustrated in a case study format. A wide variety of styles are included beginning with the simple single line sketch and progressing to the more elaborate, fully colored perspectives, and photomontages.

3 Model Simulation

Traditional techniques of model photography are combined with specialized techniques such as images produced with the model-scope and photomontages. Video is used in conjunction with large-scale simulators built especially for sequential photography of models.

4 Special Techniques

Techniques of photogrammetry record the sculptural contours of a residence. A computer and video projection system make a dynamic changing facade. Fiber optics are employed in a unique sign design, and a hologram is shown floating over its eventual site.

Contents

5 Computer Graphics

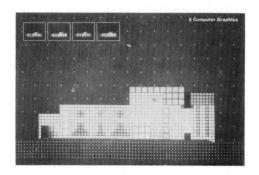

The techniques made possible by using the computer as a presentation medium are described. Some are relatively simple, such as computer graphics painting programs. Others are more complex such as perspective walkarounds and three-dimensional solid modeling techniques.

6 Computer Presentations

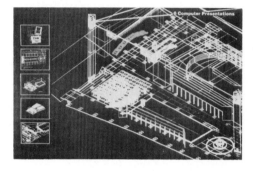

The computer is used here to display designs in a case study format. Projects show a wide variety of applications, wire frame layering techniques, and wire frame walkthrough sequences. One project involved digitizing an entire city, which is now part of an urban database.

7 Sequential Simulation

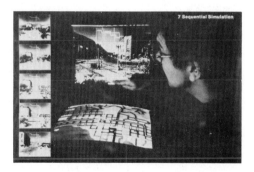

The combination of techniques shows traditional film and video trips through models, in a sequential storyboard manner. Also shown is an exotic, large-scale videodisc project wherein travel through an entire town is simulated through a computer and videodisc simulation.

8 Completed Projects

The emphasis is on the comparison between the original presentation drawing or model, and the completed project. Since the main purpose of any simulation is to describe what the project or building will look like, the comparison is made by the viewpoints illustrated.

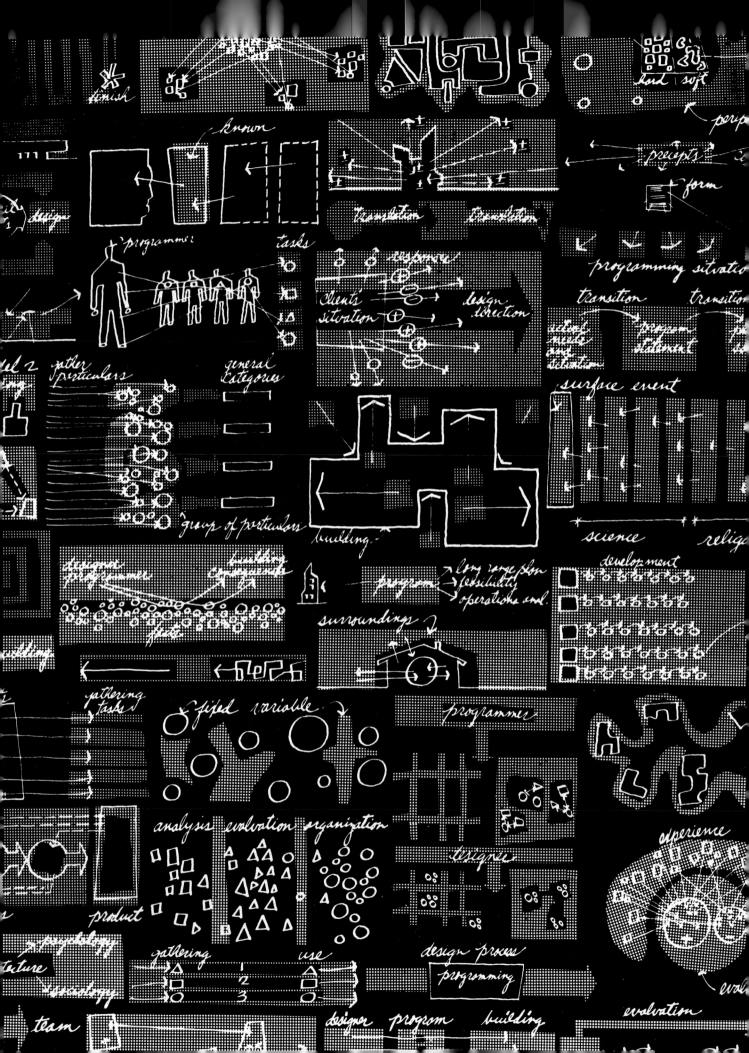

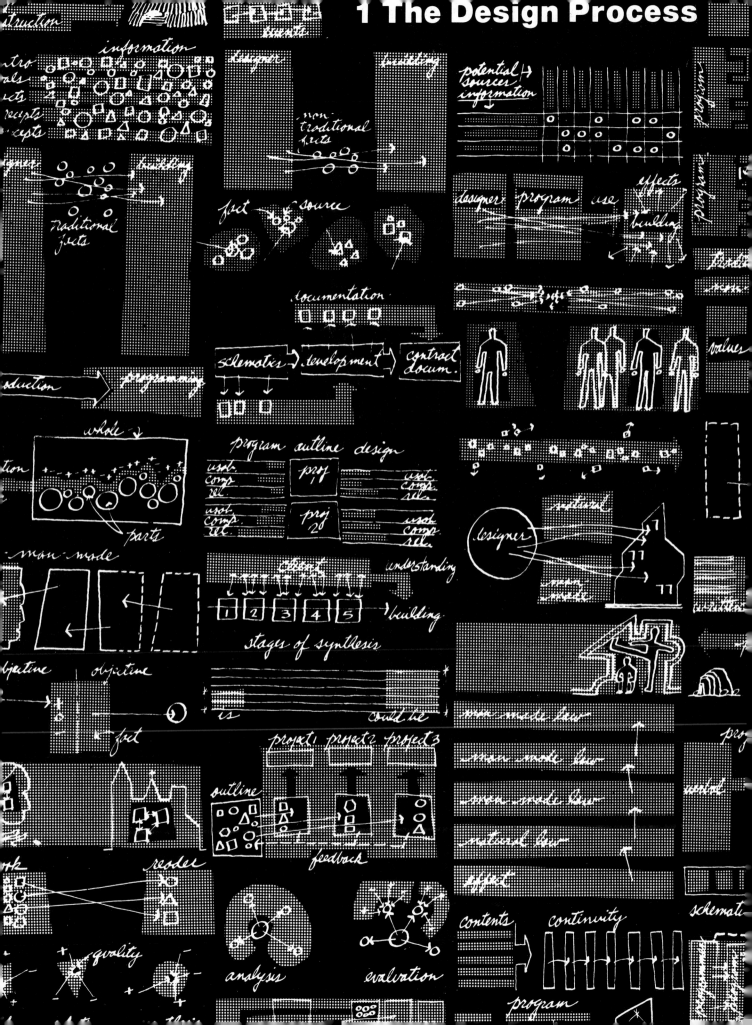

Programming

Before facilities are constructed it is important that they be designed and placed so as not to jeopardize future development, and that they relate to surrounding site constraints. Usually a total scheme is necessary to ensure that individual buildings within the project are coordinated.

This form of programming a master plan deals with such issues as optimum site use, functional building placement, efficient pedestrian and vehicular circulation, both on and off the property. As in this study for a master plan for Cochise College in Arizona, specific issues are identified. As specific buildings within the project are undertaken, each must begin with an architectural program that defines in detail what the requirements of the facility will be. Then each space is analyzed for needed furniture and equipment, personnel to be housed, and needed proximity to other areas.

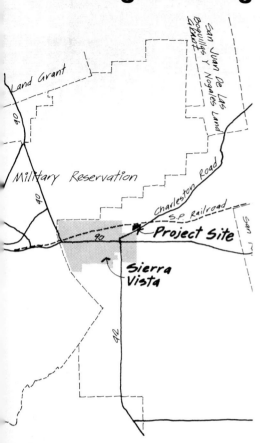

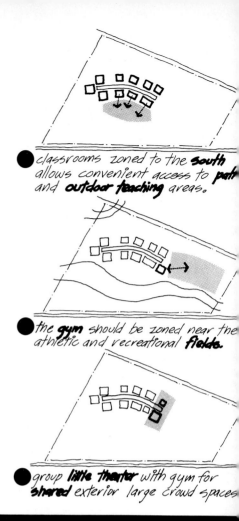

● classrooms zoned to the **south** allows convenient access to *path* and **outdoor teaching** areas.

● the **gym** should be zoned near the athletic and recreational **fields**.

● group **little theater** with gym for **shared** exterior large crowd spaces

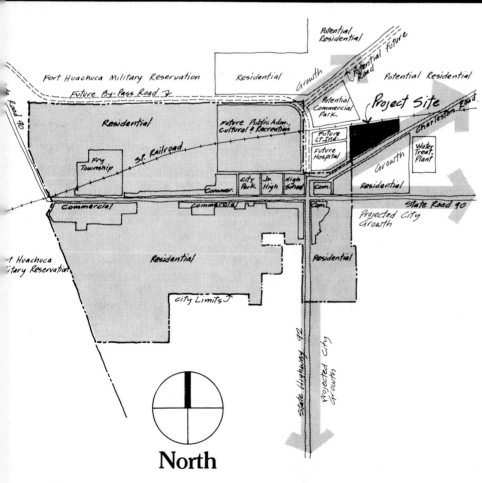

North

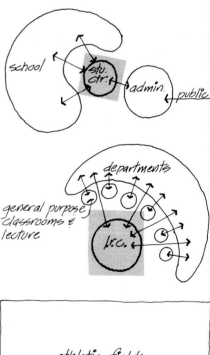

school   stu. ctr.   admin.   public

departments

general purpose classrooms & lecture

l.r.c.

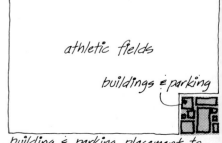

athletic fields

buildings & parking

building & parking placement to allow **flexible** field development

dministration should be the first
uilding encountered on entering
*t the **front door** of the scheme.*

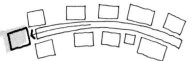

*he **student center** should terminate
and anchor the mall.*

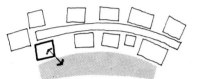

*he **learning resource center** should
have access to outdoor reading areas,
free of vehicular interference.*

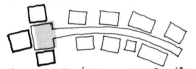

*nlarge mall at **commons** functions
for increased circulation and
principal scheme **focus**.*

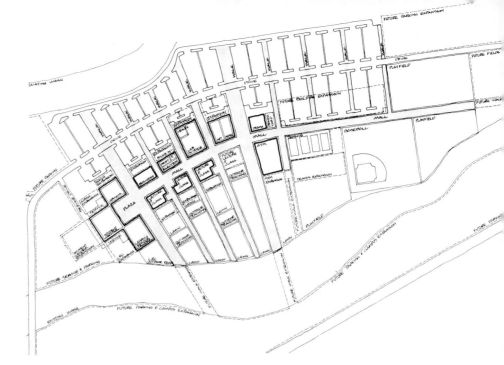

A final site plan shows the
outcome of the programming
factors in the arrangement and
placement of the structures.
The actual design of the facilities translates the information
first into schematic building
concepts and ultimately into a
detailed building design.

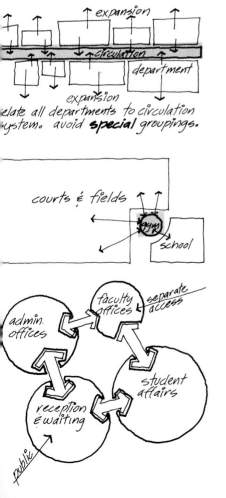

*elate all departments to circulation
system. avoid **special** groupings.*

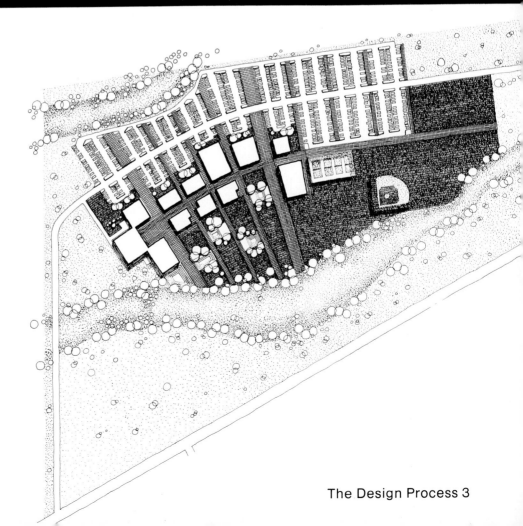

Orientation

This firm believes that the best architectural solution that can be provided is one that is generated from the many specific needs of the client. The process of orientation (understanding the components) to a new problem is practically one hundred percent of the solution.

Architectural and planning problems are comprised of a myriad of subproblems, most of which affect cost, time, convenience, and environment.

By recognizing and documenting these subproblems the architect and client are able to see and recognize relationships and alternatives.

Subproblems can provide a "record" of the development of the eventual solution, which can be shown and easily understood by anyone at any time (during or after project completion).

It is important to provide a format into which anyone can contribute. Throughout the process of identifying and recognizing the viable options for relevant subproblems, all of the information has to be equally weighted. However, at the conclusion of the information-gathering stage, priorities become the final determinant of the appropriateness of singular options to each subproblem. Various points of view can be emphasized, certain goals weighted more, and a single solution emerges which clearly defines all aspects of the problem by combining the most appropriate options.

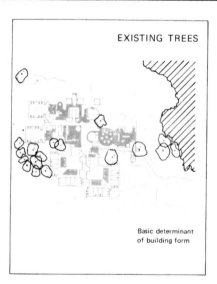

EXISTING TREES

Basic determinant of building form

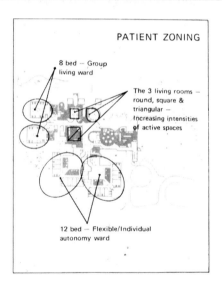

PATIENT ZONING

8 bed — Group living ward

The 3 living rooms — round, square & triangular — increasing intensities of active spaces

12 bed — Flexible/Individual autonomy ward

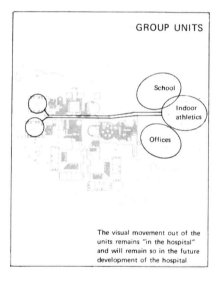

GROUP UNITS

School

Indoor athletics

Offices

The visual movement out of the units remains "in the hospital" and will remain so in the future development of the hospital

ZONING

Future School

enclosed play   open play

To Road & Town

Future Office

Children/Staff Mix

Children's World

Symbolic Movement Toward Community from most protective areas by sequential zones of increasing involvement with others

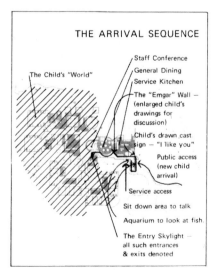

THE ARRIVAL SEQUENCE

The Child's "World"

Staff Conference
General Dining
Service Kitchen
The "Emgar" Wall — (enlarged child's drawings for discussion)
Child's drawn cast sign — "I like you"
Public access (new child arrival)
Service access
Sit down area to talk
Aquarium to look at fish.
The Entry Skylight — all such entrances & exits denoted

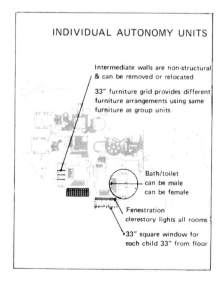

INDIVIDUAL AUTONOMY UNITS

Intermediate walls are non-structural & can be removed or relocated

33" furniture grid provides different furniture arrangements using same furniture as group units

Bath/toilet can be male can be female

Fenestration clerestory lights all rooms

33" square window for each child 33" from floor

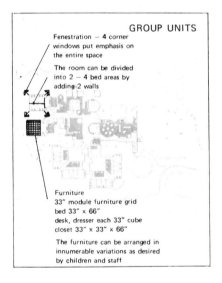

GROUP UNITS

Fenestration — 4 corner windows put emphasis on the entire space

The room can be divided into 2 – 4 bed areas by adding 2 walls

Furniture
33" module furniture grid
bed 33" x 66"
desk, dresser each 33" cube
closet 33" x 33" x 66"

The furniture can be arranged in innumerable variations as desired by children and staff

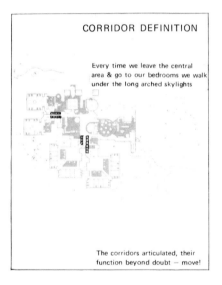

CORRIDOR DEFINITION

Every time we leave the central area & go to our bedrooms we walk under the long arched skylights

The corridors articulated, their function beyond doubt — move!

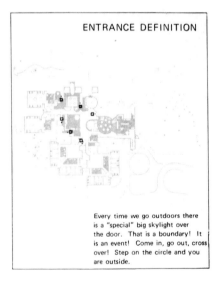

ENTRANCE DEFINITION

Every time we go outdoors there is a "special" big skylight over the door. That is a boundary! It is an event! Come in, go out, cross over! Step on the circle and you are outside.

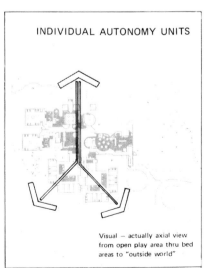

INDIVIDUAL AUTONOMY UNITS

Visual — actually axial view from open play area thru bed areas to "outside world"

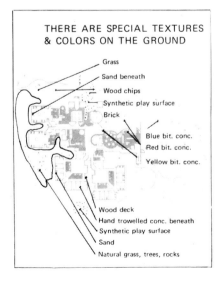

THERE ARE SPECIAL TEXTURES & COLORS ON THE GROUND

Grass
Sand beneath
Wood chips
Synthetic play surface
Brick
Blue bit. conc.
Red bit. conc.
Yellow bit. conc.

Wood deck
Hand trowelled conc. beneath
Synthetic play surface
Sand
Natural grass, trees, rocks

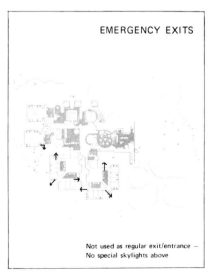

EMERGENCY EXITS

Not used as regular exit/entrance — No special skylights above

ISSUES	INVENTORY	GOALS	CRITERIA/CONSTRAINTS	OPTIONS
SITE CIRCULATION				
DELIVERY				
PARKING				
RECREATION SPACE				
FORMAL ORGANIZATION				
LOCATION of DINING FACILITY				
LANDSCAPE				

CORE FACILITIES DEVELOPMENT AND SITE PLAN

ISSUES	INVENTORY	GOALS	CRITERIA/CONSTRAINTS	OPTIONS
LOCATION				
DELIVERY SYSTEMS				
FOOD PREPARATION				
SERVING AREA				
DINING				
ACCESS				
FLEXIBILITY				

KITCHEN · DINING FACILITY

Methodology

The vehicle for this firm's process is called "The Wall" simply because all information relevant to the problem is posted on a large wall in the office. They continually analyze and structure their thinking on the wall surface, refining random thoughts into a more ordered "information field."

Wall One marked the development of the schematic design. Wall Two represents the development of a formal expression of the design.

The schematic design was the starting point for Wall Two, whereby basic functional relationships were made more explicit and a spatial program was established. The problem was to generate a formal language to express the activities and feelings of the users as defined in the schematic design phase.

They identified basic formal issues: program components, environmental quality, and architectural surfaces. Each of these issues was broken into subproblems, each of which could be solved in various ways.

Using their computer, they found the most compatible combinations of the most critical parameters. They then used the highest scoring combination as the basis for choosing appropriate options from the remaining parameters. The formal solution, then, is the combination of subsolutions indicated by the profile lines drawn from item to item.

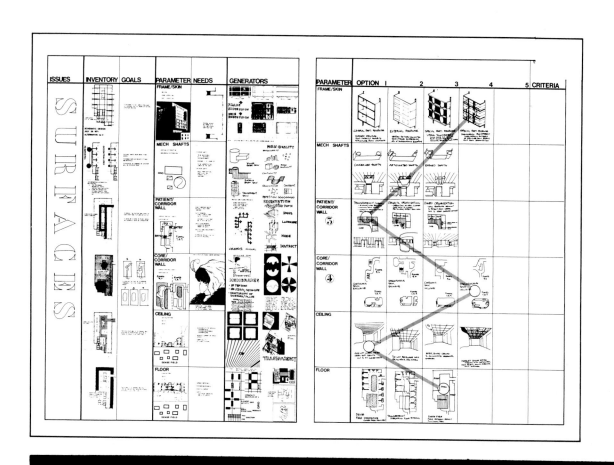

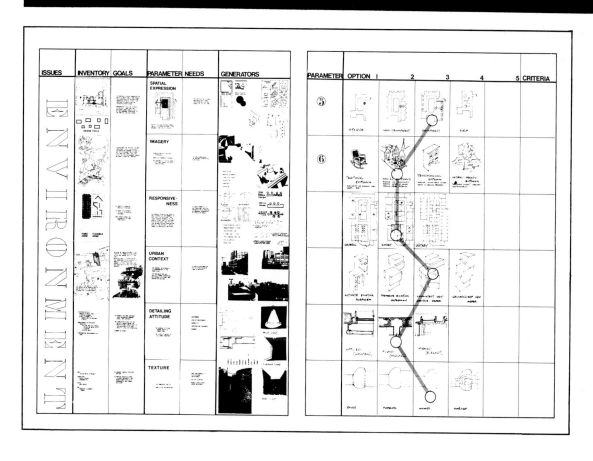

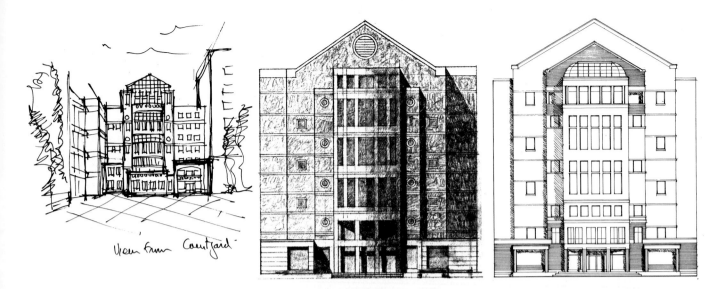

view from courtyard

Design Process

This firm describes the design process as one of discovery by its nature. You learn a little about one aspect of a building and it teaches you something about another, and the design is modified to accommodate it. Often, these aspects involve an interplay between technical and human issues.

The early drawings of the south facade were thought of as being one-dimensional and the first drawing was formal enough to be a baroque church. The portholes alluded to forms found on other campus buildings. The pediment was based on the incorrect assumption that the entire mechanical system would sit on top.

The small sketches deal with the emergence of a need for a greenhouse and a director's suite below. The greenhouse provides the building with a crystal-like crown. The sketch has figures like parapets. Its medieval look finally seemed simply eccentric and was dropped out. The last sketch resolves the greenhouse treatment. The plan view studies make the need obvious. This drawing also concludes the studies of sun shading for the windows. The facade sketches study how to use the exterior material, terra cotta.

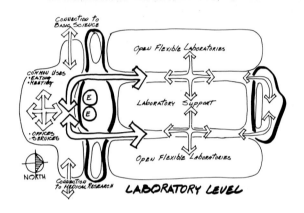

LABORATORY LEVEL

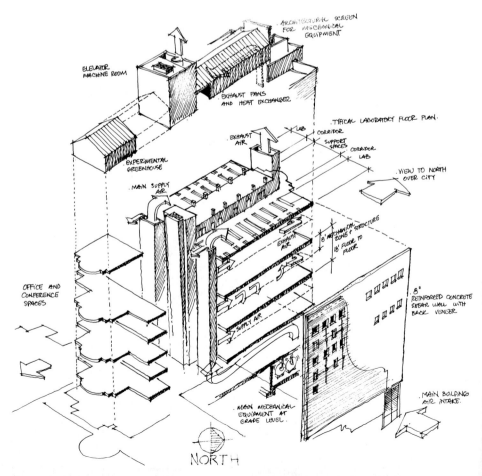

NORTH

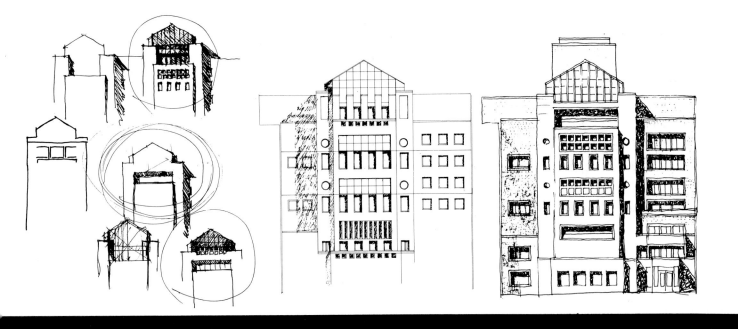

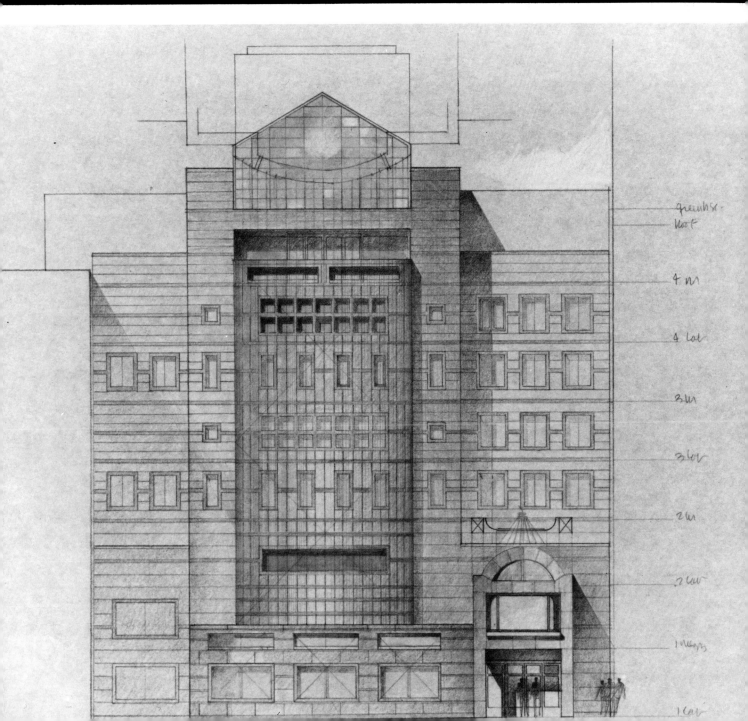

greenhse
roof

4 n

4 lot

3 n

3 lot

2 n

2 lot

1 meeps

1 lot

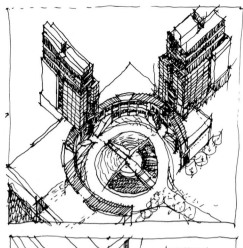

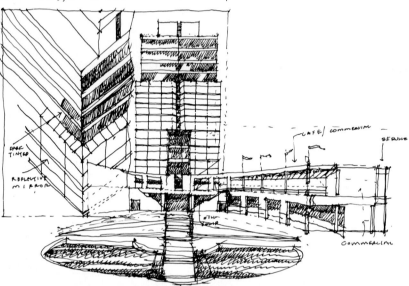

Concept Sketches

This series of preliminary concept sketches was executed for an urban commercial development. They were part of the process of developing the architectural variations for a site plan that remained unchanged in concept. Once a perspective vantage point was selected, the sketches were all done from the same location. This provided a basis for comparison of the designs that led to the final proposed scheme.

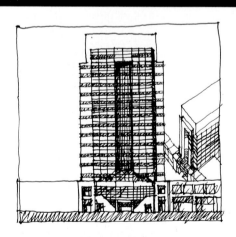

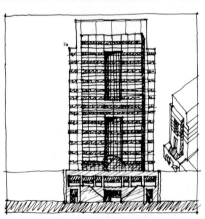

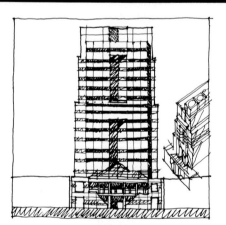

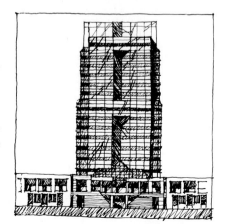

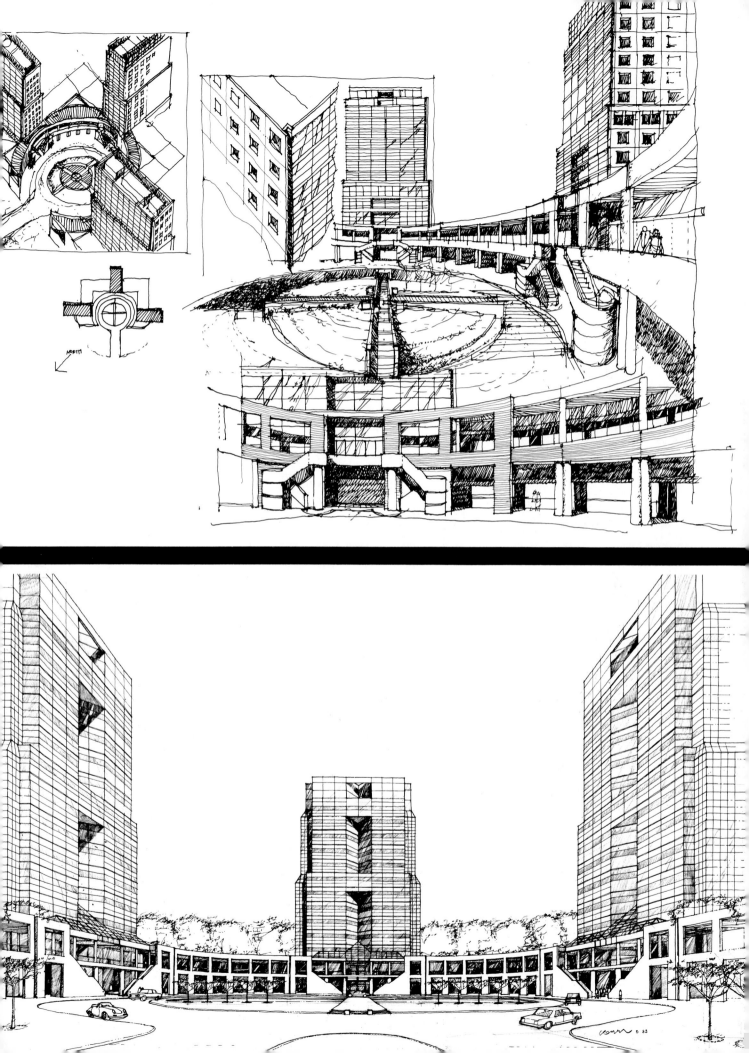

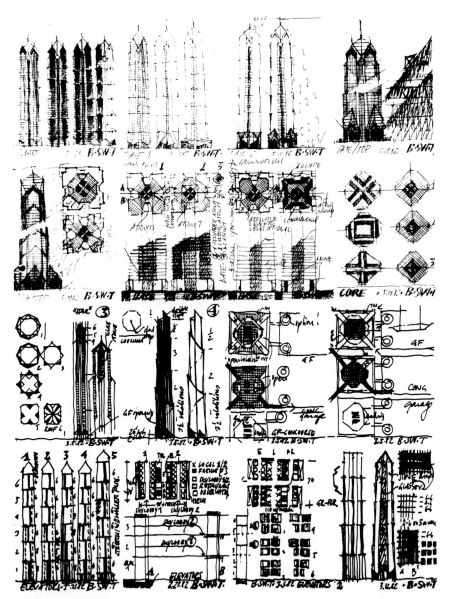

Design Studies

The illustrations here represent the beginning of the drawing process for the building. This process is important for this architect, who prefers not to start with a fixed concept. He considers options and solves problems in the process of drawing. In designing this tower, he made thousands of sketches, starting with a program and coming up with a design technology. The process of drawing is integral with the process of conceptualizing.

The first series of drawings shows all the possible configurations. From these, several were selected for study and were then developed further.

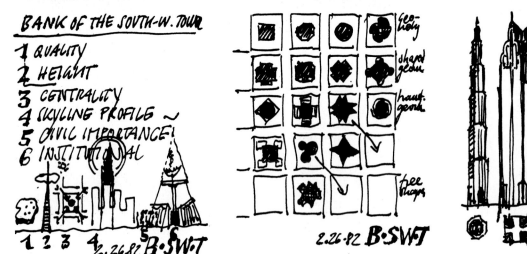

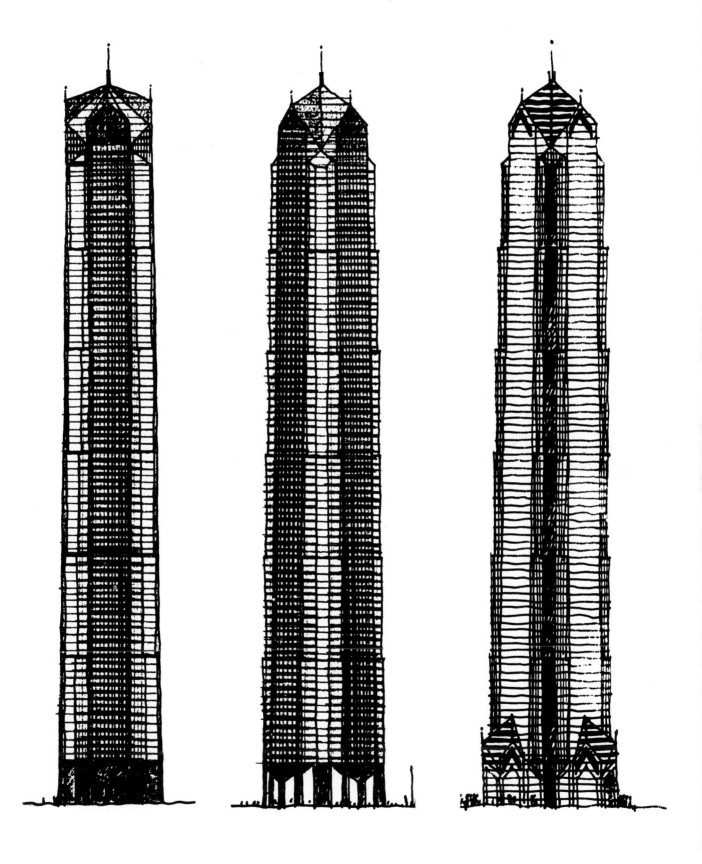

COUPE RESTAUREE DU TEMPLE D'ASCLEPIOS

FACADE RESTAUREE DU TEMPLE D'ASCLEPIOS

COUPE RESTAUREE DE LA THOLOS

16

Prix-de-Rome

These elaborate renderings of ancient Greek sites were produced in the nineteenth and early twentieth centuries by France's most gifted young architects, winners of the coveted Prix de Rome. This prize, presented to one architectural student each year by the prestigious Ecole des Beaux-Arts in Paris, granted the winner five years of study and travel abroad. From 1720, when the prize was initiated, award-winners went to Italy. During the fourth year of their residence abroad, each architect was required to execute a two-part Envoi (a major drawing project), which was submitted to the Ecole in Paris where it was exhibited, critiqued, and then made the property of the French government. The first section of this assignment consisted of archeologically accurate drawings of an extant ancient monument. The second section, executed in the same scale and size as the first, was an imaginary, idealized re-creation of the same antique site.

The painstaking draftsmanship of these studies is the result of the rigorous training these young architects received at the Ecole des Beaux-Arts, the school that made Paris the world center of architectural training in the second half of the nineteenth century.

The factual, precise drawings of classical monuments that the students produced as the first part of their Envois proved to be important documents for archeologists. Often Prix de Rome winners worked closely with archeologists, in many instances carefully measuring edifices and recording excavations. The second part of the Envoi — the imaginary restoration of a classical site — gave architects license to be bold and fanciful in their conceptions. After 1881, these restoration drawings outnumbered the factual ones.

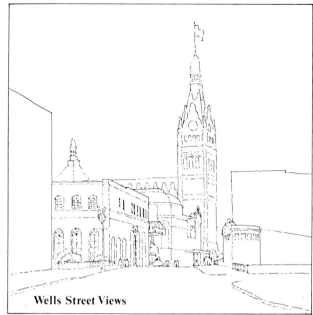

Wells Street Views

Theater District

This project created a new theater district by reusing two existing power company buildings and upgrading an existing theater. The complex was adjacent to the existing Performing Arts Center.

The urban design analysis resulted in establishing site development criteria and site utilization parameters. The proposed arcade system has a main axis presenting major access to the Fine Arts Building and the Performing Arts Center at opposite ends.

Another spine connects the arcade to City Hall Plaza on the east, and still another link at right angles gives access through a public concourse to a plaza fronting the Milwaukee River.

The simple style of illustration of both the new project and its surroundings gives a clear impression of the space without overemphasizing either the new or the old structure. Using a series of views, a walkaround adds to the impressionistic explanation of the space.

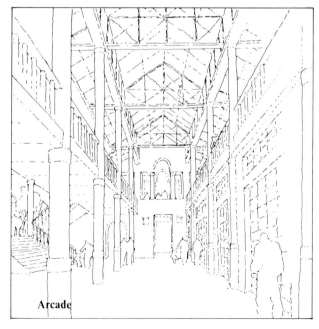

Arcade

Kilbourn Avenue Views

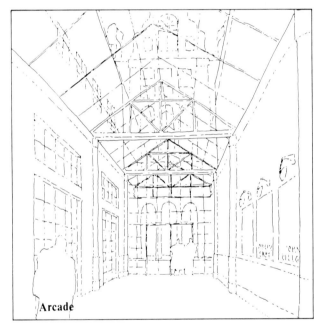

Arcade

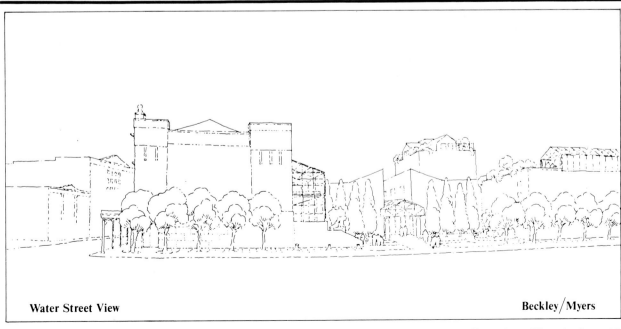

Water Street View

Beckley/Myers

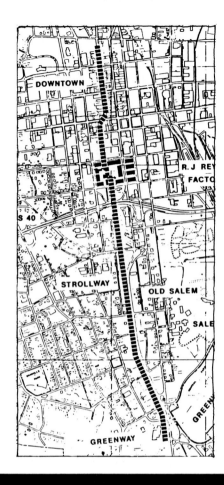

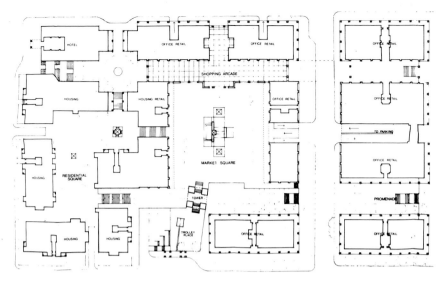

Gateway Plaza

In Winston-Salem, North Carolina, the CBD will get a new look with this proposed mixed-use plan. The fully developed scheme will include office space, retail stores, and residential units.

The freehand sketches display a human-scale viewpoint of the development. Another series of design studies, showing aerial views of the overall project, was produced on a computer. The series of views depicted here emphasizes the pedestrians' access to and use of the development.

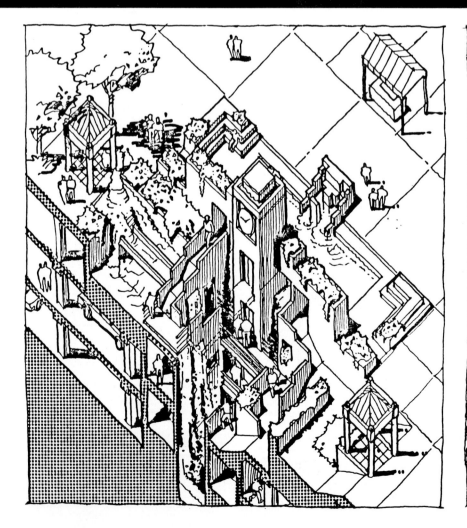

California Center

These loose environmental sketches were prepared to illustrate an entry in a competition for the Bunker Hill project in downtown Los Angeles. The project was slated for the last remaining major parcel of land in the downtown area. The emphasis of the series of drawings was placed on depicting pedestrians' views as they toured the mixed-use project, which features residential, commercial, and retail uses. The focal point of the project was the entertainment center, which is shown in several of the sketches.

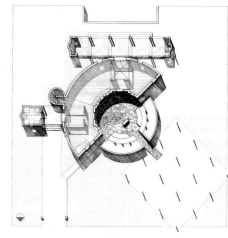

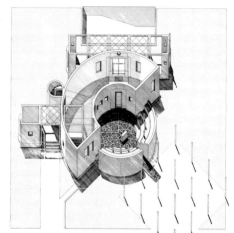

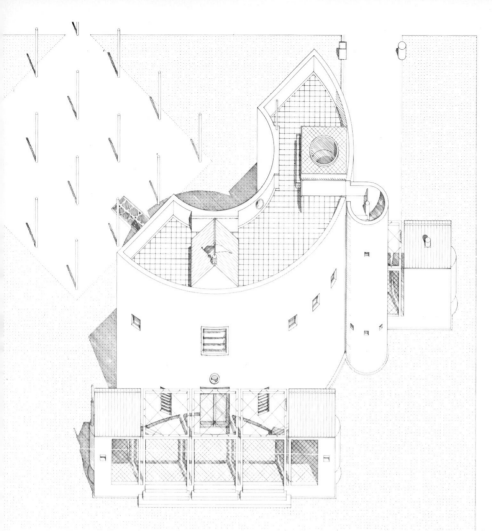

Healy House

A variety of presentation techniques is used to describe this small rural house designed for a young horticulturist. In the series of drawings, several layers of space are delineated. This same technique is utilized in a series of photographs of an abstract model in plan view. The large axonometric utilizes hidden lines and cutaway techniques to show space within the building.

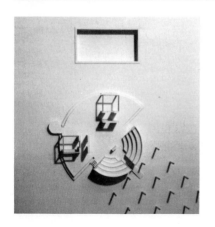

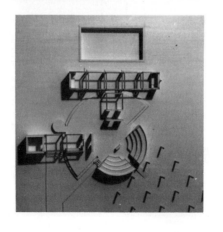

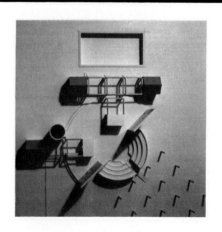

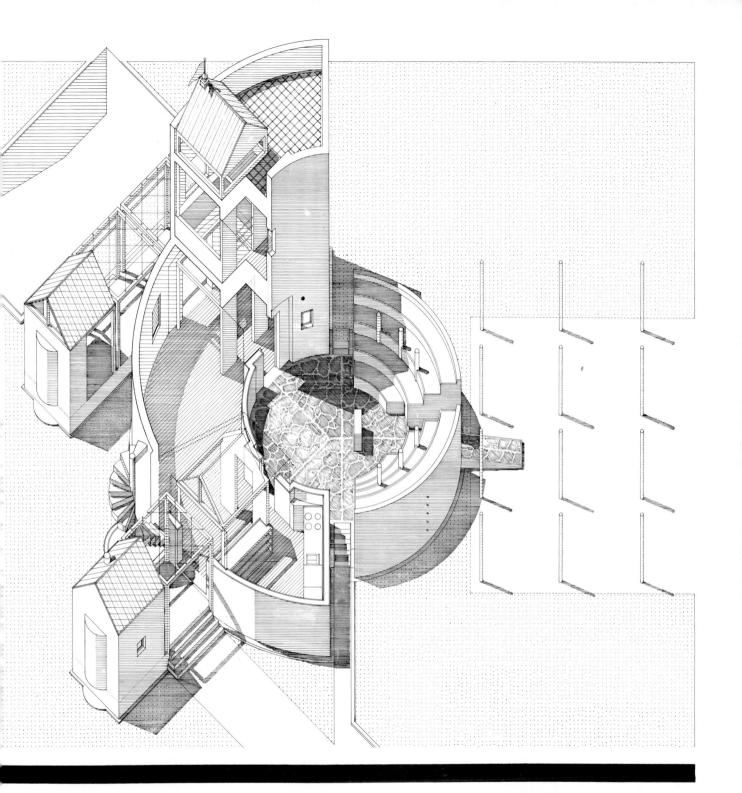

Kiva Sports Center

From the overall view to the closest detail, this series has a consistency of style and technique that gives it a realistic feeling. Attention to detail and the use of appropriate surroundings make each view very realistic in feeling. The exterior skating rink in winter becomes the pool in summer. The overall ambiance created within each sketch makes it all the more believable.

Solar-Ray

Selection of viewpoint and use of the circular format provide a distinctive touch to these drawings. They are executed in colored pencil using a very delicate style of drawing. The shapes and materials are defined by color rather than by outline which is then filled in with color.

Phillips Petroleum

Consolidation of work force was the reason for this headquarters structure. The emphasis in the series of drawings was therefore placed on the employees' work spaces, conference rooms, and lobby spaces. The loose style of drawing produces an openness to the interior views.

Phillips Point

The technique used to depict this mixed-use development was a series of ink sketches. The freehand drawing is done over a conventionally plotted perspective or over a perspective that is computer-generated. Since the time frame for these developmental drawings is short, the technique must be simple and direct. An overall view is always done to show the whole development. Then several smaller views from the ground level emphasize the entourage and establish the proper setting for the proposed new environment.

Kellogg's

Freehand pen-and-ink sketches were used to depict the environmental quality of the interior spaces of this corporate headquarters office building. Emphasis was placed on the public spaces.

SANTA CLARA STREET
MAINE STREET
MAINE STREET

MARINA VISTA WAY

PARCEL A   PARCEL B

MARINA VISTA WAY

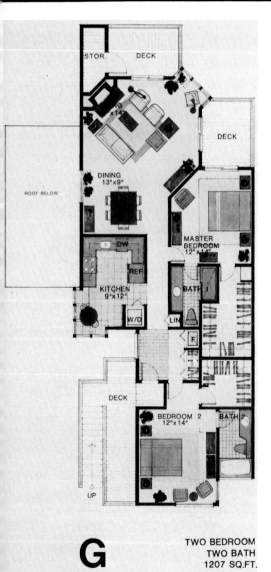

STOR.   DECK

ROOF BELOW

DINING
13'x9'

DECK

DW

REF

KITCHEN
9'x12'

W/D

MASTER
BEDROOM
12'x14'

BATH 1

LIN

DECK

BEDROOM 2
12'x14'

BATH 2

UP

G

TWO BEDROOM
TWO BATH
1207 SQ.FT.

SCALE: 0 2 4 8

36

Housing Project

Design development drawings can be effectively combined with sketches and floor plans for a more complete presentation of a project. Here the site plan displays the overall coverage of the lot and shows the configuration of the dwelling units. The extended elevational view above was developed from the ortho- graphic drawings, which show everything in a flat plane. Shadows and tonal rendition help give it a three-dimensional look. The full-perspective sketches provide the most representative views of the project. These are all supplemented by the rendered floor plans, where color and texture produce a more realistic image.

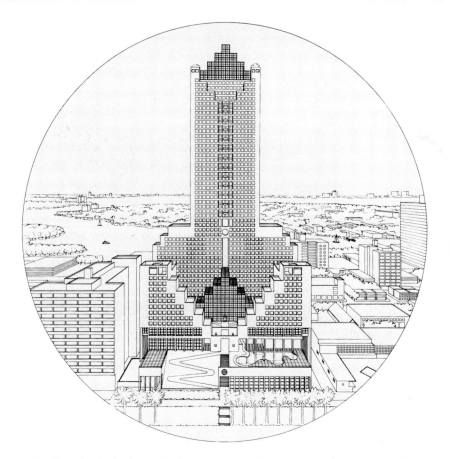

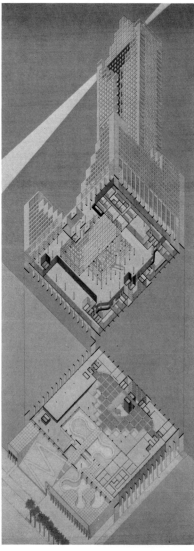

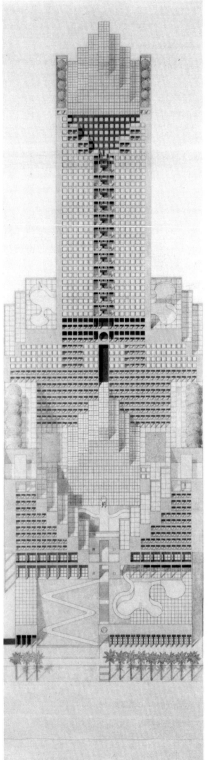

Miami Hotel

Unique viewpoints and techniques are combined to depict this proposed hotel building. The line drawings in the circular format use a more traditional architectural treatment, whereas the same view below becomes elongated with the axonometric treatment of depth. The middle view below shows a cutaway, with the lower portion folded down away from the viewer and the upper portion projected up from the viewer. The main drawing in this series is a view of an enclosed courtyard executed in colored pencil.

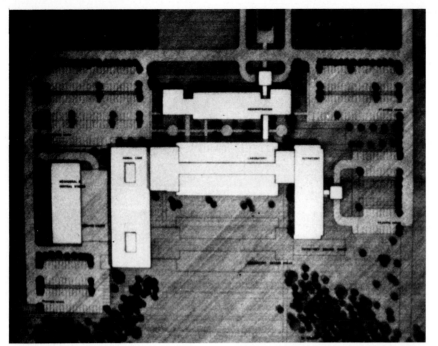

Biomedical Center

These represent steps in a diagrammatic process of turning program areas into a finished architectural project. The elements outlined in the program are transferred to model form to help establish three-dimensional relationships. The rough study models are used to illustrate the phasing of the project. Sketch renderings are created using the models as a base. Additional drawings include a cross-sectional view, in perspective, which depicts the interior spaces and mechanical and structural system.

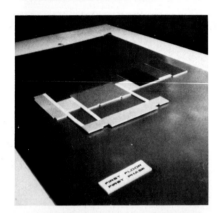

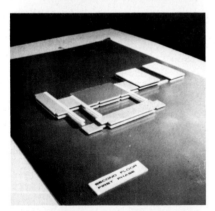

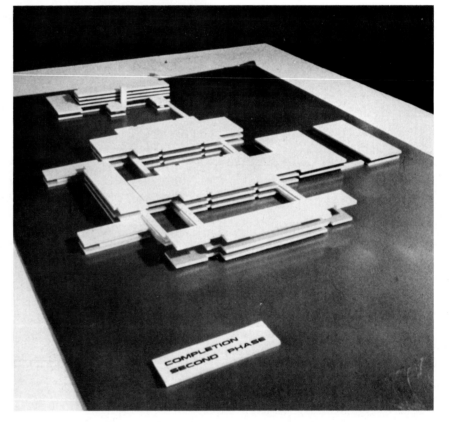

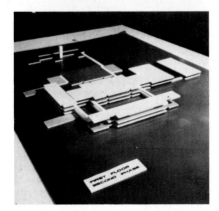

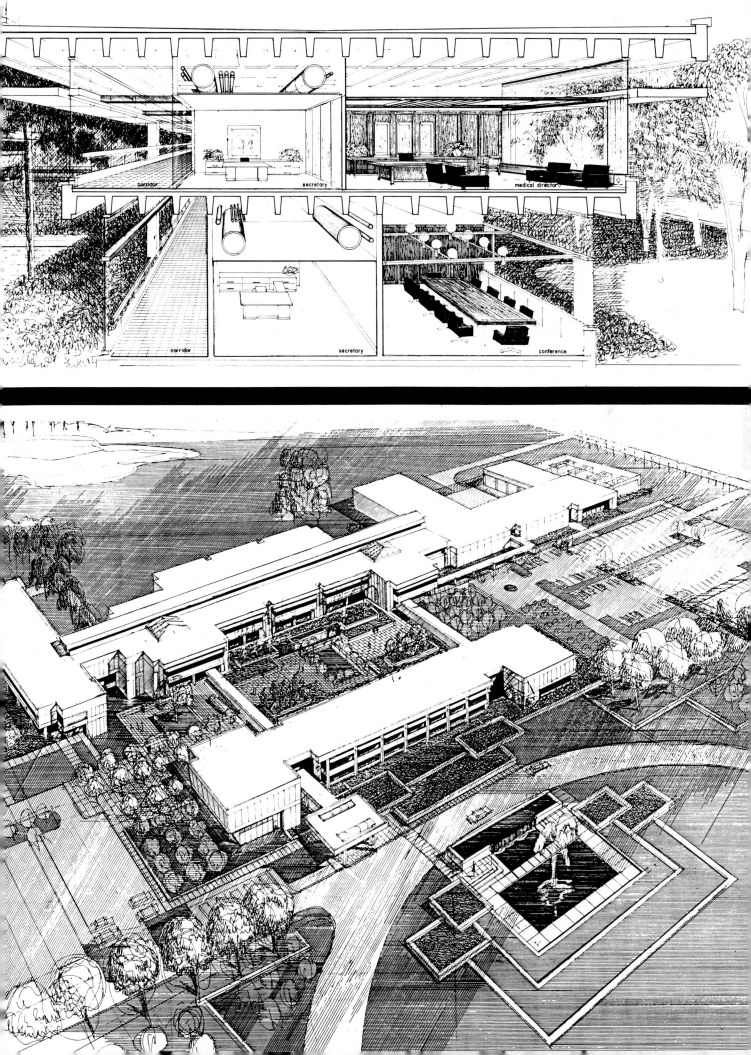

corridor   secretary   medical director

corridor   secretary   conference

175 Water Street

There is a wide difference between model photography and perspective rendering. Model photography has the advantages of choice of viewpoint and almost unlimited variations of distance and height from the building. A rendering is usually done from one fixed position because of the elaborate methods necessary to plot and draw one viewpoint.

The advantage of the drawing over the model is in the technique of delineating colors and materials with any amount of detail and texture. By comparison to this, the close-up view of a model without a lot of built-in detail looks flat. The two views of the same project illustrate the comparison. In the drawing, foreground elements are easy to work with. In the model photo, foreground detail is distracting and unrealistic.

Lower Broadway

Another technique (shown opposite) involving models is the superimposition of the model photo or rendering onto the actual site. This requires special techniques of photography, particularly if the viewpoint happens to be a converging perspective. Special care has to be taken to shoot the model from the exact same vantage point as the aerial photo was taken.

When a large-format camera such as a 4x5 or 8x10 is used, the ground glass of the camera provides an easy means of aligning the two views. By simply tracing the size and perspective convergence on the glass, you can move the camera into perfect alignment with the model.

When the image of the model coincides with the image drawn on the ground glass, the two views will be coordinated.

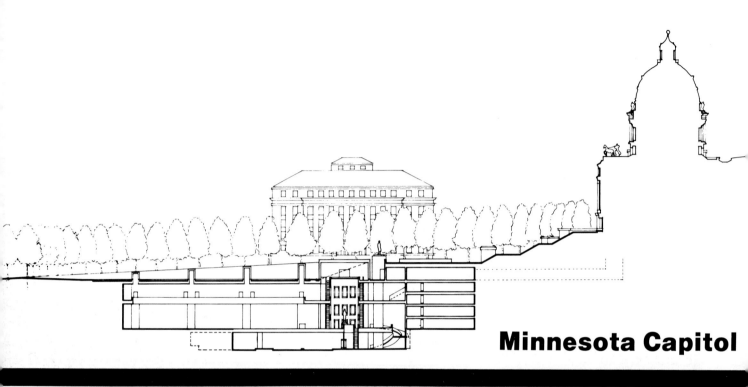

Minnesota Capitol

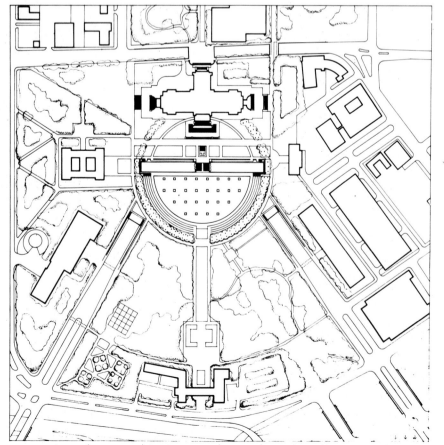

The state-initiated national competition for new facilities called for an unprecedented building type: legislative offices and a new state historical museum combined in a structure completely underground.

The proposal joins these three existing structures in a long skylit hall, which serves as a common lobby and light source. All new functions are organized along this great hall, which is itself formed into a compressed allegorical account of the state's history.

The drawing and cutaway model show the relationship of the underground public hallway to the other spaces. The ceiling has a cover of frosted glass, reminiscent of the great ice sheets that once crossed the state. Light is provided to the interior spaces by light columns protruding above the surface. At night they provide the landscape lighting. This court would be flooded with water during the summer.

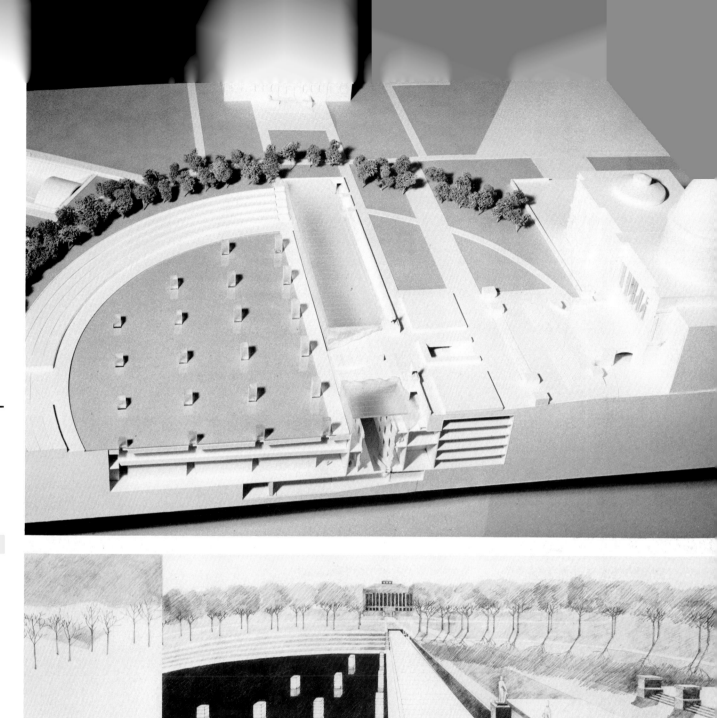

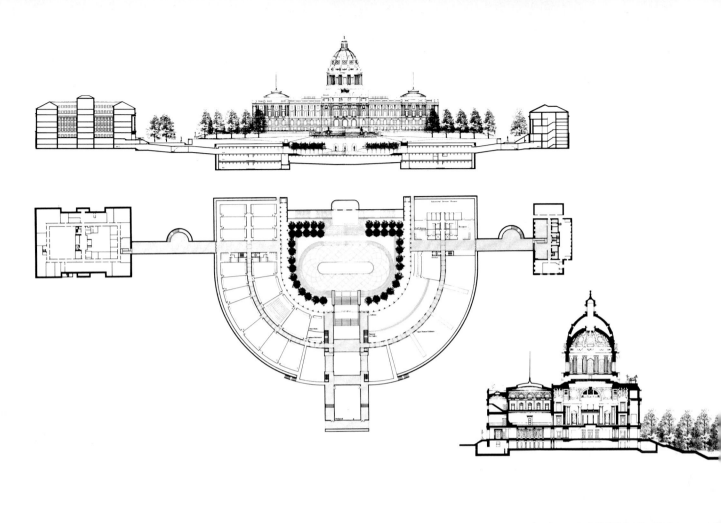

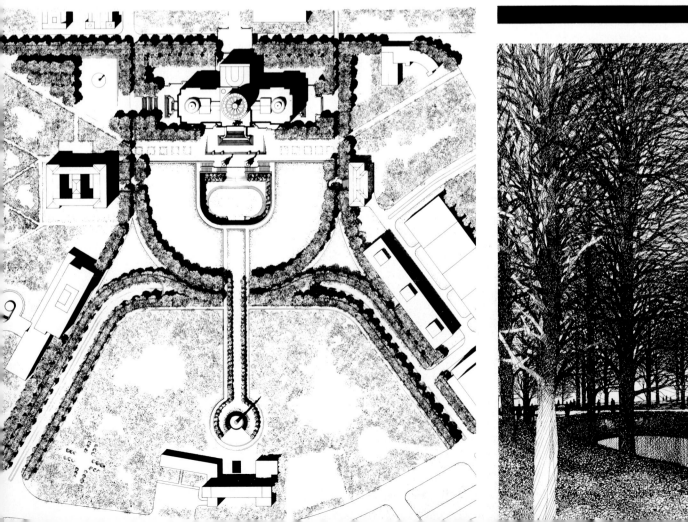

Minnesota Capital

The presentation for this second-place finalist utilized a combination of highly stylized plans and landscaped sections combined with highly detailed perspective drawings. The plan for this underground addition to the state capitol, producing a new museum and state legislative offices, offers a large landscaped area on top of the new spaces. The vehicular drive shown in the sketch is provided for access to underground parking. The technique of pen-and-ink sketches toned with overlapping textures precisely controlled the values within the drawing.

Minnesota Capitol

One of the views created from the existing building would be over the newly landscaped gardens and lawns featuring native-grown specimen trees. This view would terminate with an obelisk, which had been suggested as part of the capitol scheme years earlier by architect Cass Gilbert. Two interior views are shown. The one that links the existing building with the new structure shows the same statue that is shown in the top view.

Four model photographs, all taken from the exact camera angle, show four levels of the underground space. The model was lit primarily by one main light source to provide definition to the interior partitioned spaces and to the contours in the grade level shot.

Horizon Hill Center

These projects demonstrate the difference between design drawings and perspective renderings. The design drawings are usually constructed using orthographic or axonometric projection methods. If they are colored, they are usually executed with an approach that is more graphic than realistic.

Perspective renderings are primarily executed with a medium that will make the project appear as realistic as possible. In this case, the medium is opaque tempera paint. The highly reflective quality of the glass-sheathed structures is easily simulated using this technique.

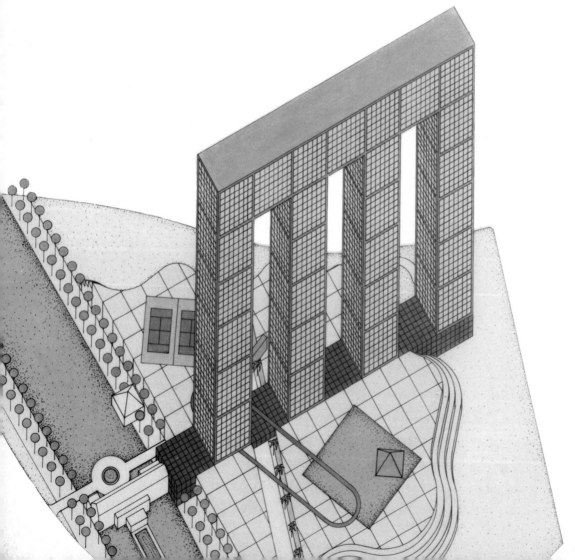

The Atlantis

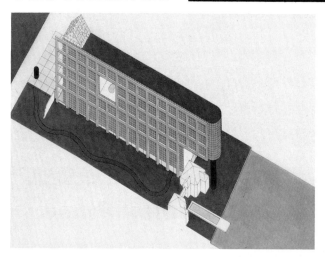 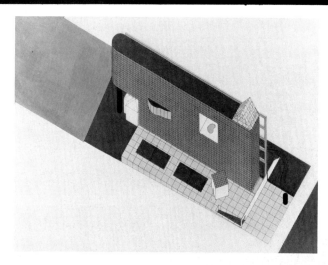

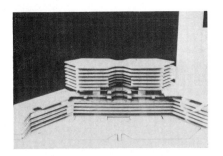

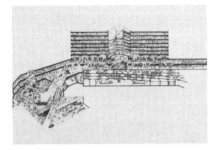

Copley Place

This series of colored renderings depicts a major new development in an urban area. The technique chosen was opaque tempera paint, because realism can be achieved easily with this medium.

A cardboard model was constructed and used as the basis for a sectional cutaway view. Other views were produced by the traditional layout methods, showing various parts of the galleria space and the central atrium space. An aerial photograph was used as the basis for a superimposed view of the building. Other ground level views depict the building in its urban setting.

Compare these drawings with photographs of the detailed interior model shown on pages 116 and 117. These model photos are later compared to the identical viewpoints of the completed project.

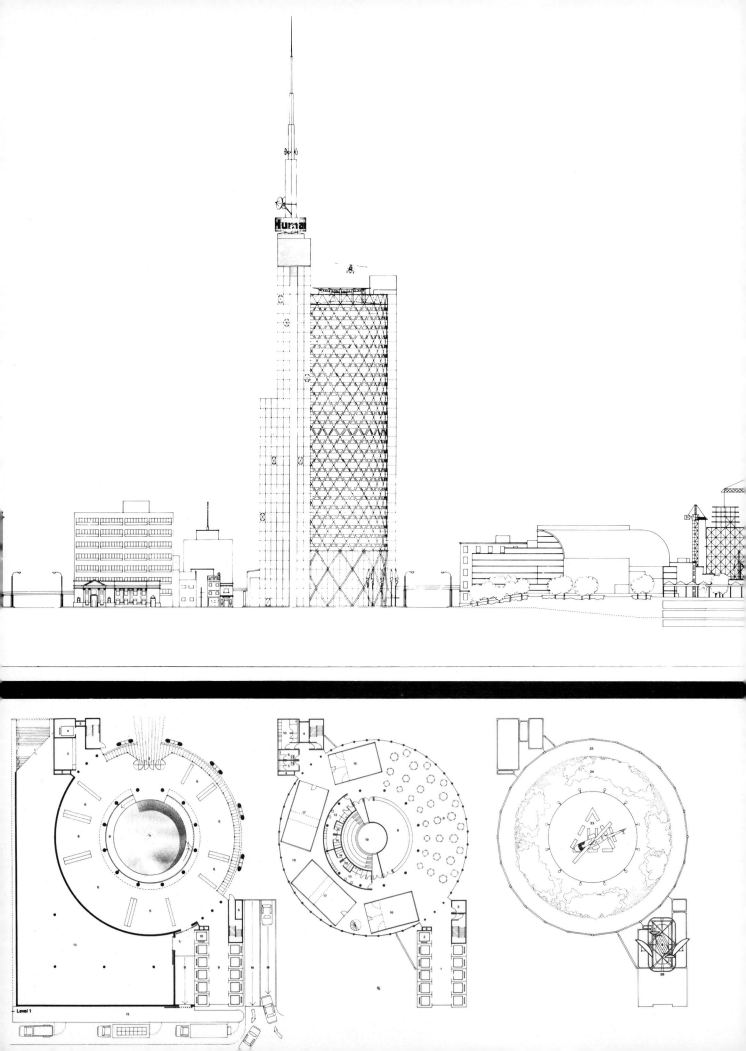

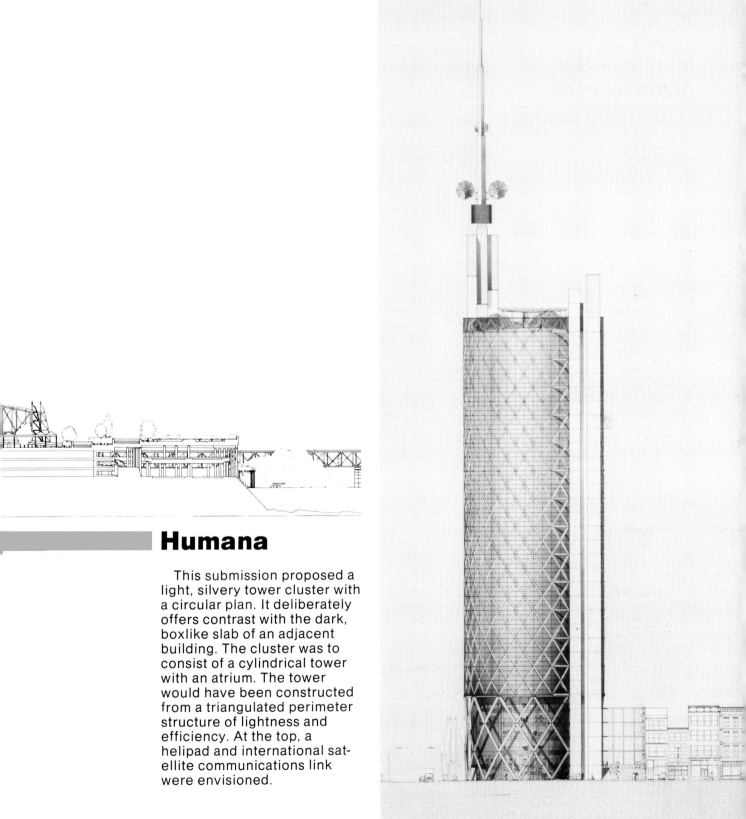

Humana

This submission proposed a light, silvery tower cluster with a circular plan. It deliberately offers contrast with the dark, boxlike slab of an adjacent building. The cluster was to consist of a cylindrical tower with an atrium. The tower would have been constructed from a triangulated perimeter structure of lightness and efficiency. At the top, a helipad and international satellite communications link were envisioned.

Vancouver Transit

This series of drawings was developed to cover a wide variety of situations involving a major new transit system for the city. Therefore, many different techniques were employed to illustrate how the system related to existing thoroughfares, structures, and neighborhoods. Since much of the system in the urban area was underground, special cutaway sections were drawn to show the relationships of the underground network to the activity above. Sectional perspectives were also used to depict how the transit system related to proposed new structures.

A combination of styles was also used depending on the intended use of the drawing. Quick sketches were made for preliminary study and review.

Vancouver Transit

Many of the station designs were drawn first in ink line and later colored with a watercolor and airbrush technique. Another technique was used to show the system in existing neighborhoods. Here, colored photos of the site were enlarged and the track and station design were painted over the photograph using opaque tempera. The techniques selected were appropriate for each situation.

60

Expo 86

The computer-generated base drawing was divided into six zones. Each of the zone drawings will provide a basis for design development, good discussion, and functions as a visual and thematic illustration of the individual zones. The drawings can also be presented as a combined 6-panel overview of the total site.

The medium of wash off mylars and large format color boards allows for updating and collaging of new images as the project develops.

Architects, landscape architects, and designers can insert design proposals on the wash off mylars for design evaluation and presentation. As these design proposals are implemented, colored prints of the drawings can be spliced into the overview drawing, providing a current view of the world's fair.

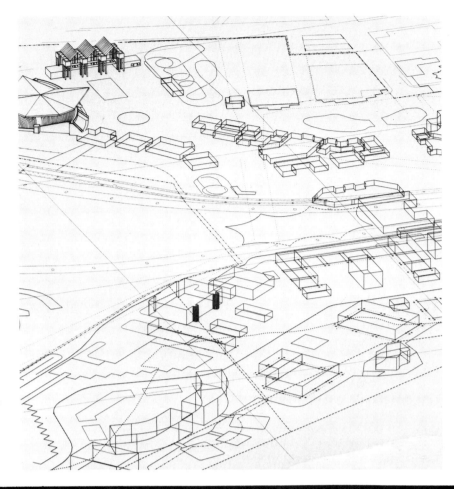

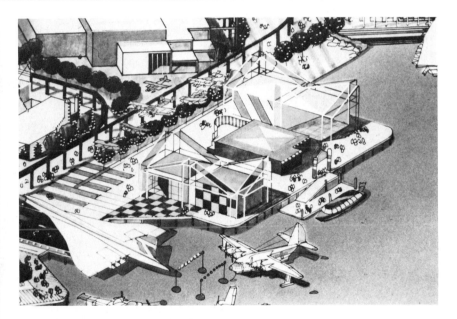

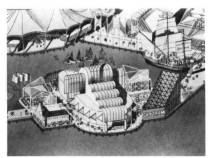

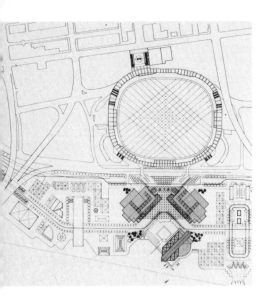

B.C. Place

A computer-generated aerial view of the city skyline, mountains, and existing stadium provided the basis for this detailed view of one of the pavilions of Expo 86. The pavilion details were plotted using traditional perspective methods. The final version is a colored drawing.

Two additional drawings show the pavilion with full activity anticipated for the world's fair, and after. Following the fair the complex will become an entertainment center featuring museums, retail space and restaurants.

B.C. Place

These drawings are part of a large series produced to depict the environmental character of a proposed major development. They worked from site photographs for reference, and sometimes from computer-generated layouts. They applied their stylistic technique over those layouts.

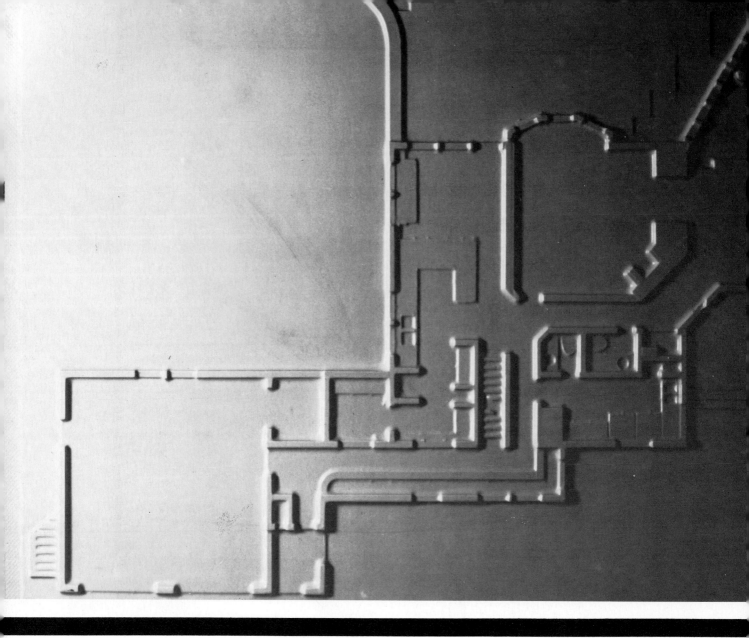

Braille House

Tactile blueprints were used to describe architectural floor plans to a blind client.

The vacuum-formed floor plan is made of 0.05-inch white polystyrene sheet. The mold is made by gluing strips of wood onto a blueprint of the building plan, which, in turn, is mounted to a sheet of cardboard. The sheet of polystyrene is mounted in a frame and heated in an oven until it is soft. The mold is placed on a vacuum table where the plastic is placed over it and drawn tightly to it by a vacuum pump.

When the plastic cools, it retains the shape of the mold. Multiple copies can be made from the same mold, and the mold can be easily modified.

Transparent Model

By adding a three-dimensional look to a typical residential floor plan, you can increase the viewer's comprehension of the space. Shallow bars are added to the floor plan layout to give it a slightly raised appearance.

Further enhancements to the residential model are seen in the view of a totally transparent scale model. This allows views into all the interior spaces from any number of angles. It also shows the relationship of all the spaces.

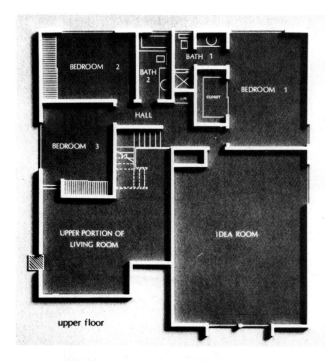

upper floor

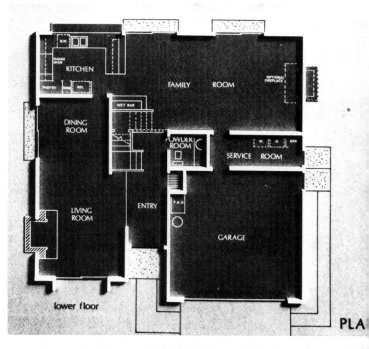

lower floor

PLA

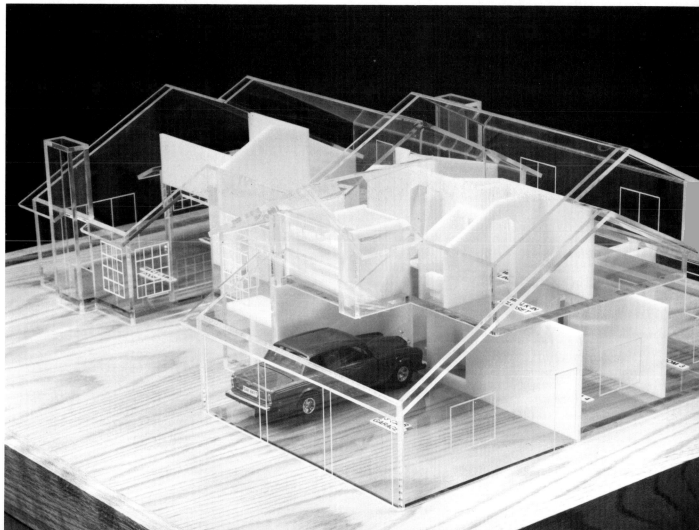

Bonn Competition

This was an entry in a design competition for the central courtyard and hotel of the general office of Telecommunication in West Germany. The development of the design was supported by various models to study design concepts, to produce presentation drawings, and to present design proposals with appropriate visualization techniques.

The initial stage set model was built to study perspective angles and the locations of pools, fountains, and other elements. Photographs of the stage model became the basis for sketches to generate perspective views of design proposals. The elevations of surrounding buildings were pasted on cardboard, cut out, and positioned according to their location on the site. Photographs were taken with a 28mm PC (perspective control) wide-angle lens positioned on the hotel terrace, simulating a view from this location into the courtyard.

The design was dominated by a star theme. Arrangements of various star sculptures functioned as ornaments and provided space for kiosks, entrances, and lobbies. The section through the courtyard on the right shows the arrangement of the various design elements. At the left of the section a star is inserted into the transparent hotel facade. A bridge, which is supported with a starlike structure, connects the hotel terrace with the platform on the courtyard. The courtyard itself is dominated by two large star sculptures, providing cover for the garage exit and kiosk.

The model shots all show details of the star sculptures, which were covered with plastic made out of diffraction grating. Different planes of the stars would give different reflections to emphasize the shape of the objects.

Another view shows the entrance to a subway. It is

crowned by a swinging star. The final view is taken from the hotel terrace and shows the bridge crossing over the pool, and the centralized star sculpture over the garage.

For this presentation it was essential to use photography as a method to simulate the effect of light on the real situation.

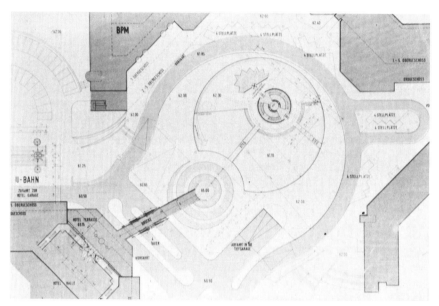

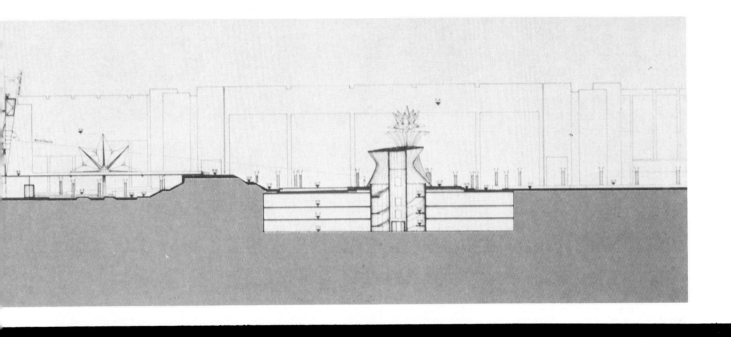

Lydell Square

This project was executed at the University of Stuttgart Department of Urban Design and Planning. Different techniques of model presentation, model documentations, and environmental documentation were investigated. The integration of sketching, photography, and video in combination with model building techniques was investigated.

The growing number of planning projects had made it necessary to find methods to visualize design concepts in forms recognizable by the architecturally untrained. An existing built environment, Lydell Square, in Karlsruhe, which was scheduled to undergo restoration, was chosen as the set.

All facades were photographed with a large-format camera to provide as much distortion-free reproduction as possible. A number of scaled photographs were printed of each facade. Cars and trees that covered parts of the facade were eliminated by pasting small pieces of photos on the wall over these areas.

The final facade collages were pasted on cardboard and assembled as a stage model. Large three-dimensional built elements, such as roof windows, were actually built as three-dimensional objects. Tedious model technique was used to present the model (for the camera) with the utmost reality. The final model was then photographed with a snorkel camera device, allowing the visual presentation of the model environment from the pedestrian's viewpoint.

The research project was accompanied by a student's course in which students were taught in different visualization techniques. For a building gap, they had to design a residential building. Various designs were inserted, and photographs were taken from the same location. This provided an excellent method for design evaluation and comparison with the existing situation.

72

Lydell Square

These photographs show how pictures taken with a special snorkel camera compare to reality. The combination of model building techniques and snorkel photography is most useful if it is desired to produce a sequential or animated walk-through. If only one view is required, it might be more feasible to just take a picture of the real environment and insert a photomontage. The emphasis during this project was sequential and dynamic simulation. The camera was held by a support system that allowed movement in all three directions. The resulting viewpoints taken with the snorkel lens are compared to photos of the actual scene.

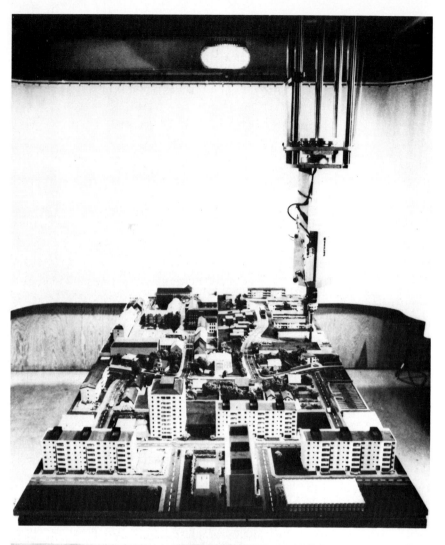

Model Simulators

Architecture, as we perceive it, is generally static. While buildings do not move and form a fixed relation with the landscape, the people who live in such an environment perceive it as a transitorial space.

Special simulation techniques were developed to study the built environment, and new methods were studied to help the architect and planner visualize sequential perception of a project before it is built.

The documentation medium has to be sequential, such as a slide series, film, or video. The planned design has to be presented in a form that simulates the actual design, such as a scale model. The viewpoint of the optic and the angle of view have to be identical with a pedestrian's or driver's view in the real world.

The development of video technology made it possible to view in real time through the videocamera, which was attached to a periscope device. This scope or snorkel located the viewpoint very close to the model surface, allowing images to be taken from a height identical to the driver's or pedestrian's eye height.

The videocamera itself is driven by stepping motors, providing movements in all three directions and controlled over a video monitor.

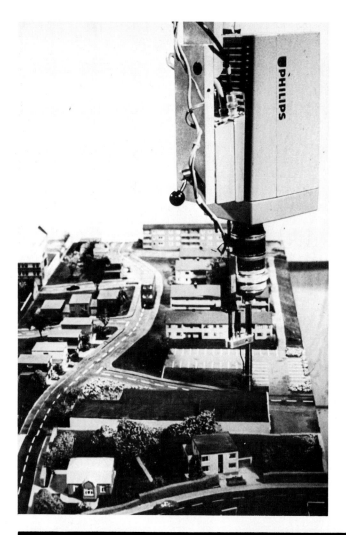

Another simple method is to use an 8mm camera with a 45-degree angled mirror. However, streets have to be as wide as the mirror, the camera has to be moved by hand very steadily, and the operator doesn't see what is being filmed. (Pictured lower left.)

Video-based simulators provide an excellent picture quality and can be equipped with a number of devices that allow control of the filming of the model.

The simulator (top left) was developed at the University of Lundt in Sweden. It is a video-camera-supported device and uses an endoscope to take the pictures. The operator controls the movements of the videocamera with a steering wheel, very similar to driving a car. Around the simulator table is a curtain providing a plain (although not very realistic) background.

Model Simulators

Holland has done extensive research in the use of video simulators. Each major architectural university has such an installation used as design support for students or for real projects helping architects, planners, and members of participatorial design projects to find better solutions.

The simulator (top left) installed in Delft is used mainly by students for support in residential planning. The model is built out of wooden building blocks. Facades were silk screened on self-sticking material which was simply pasted on the wooden blocks.

The design school in Wageningen has not only a very sophisticated simulator installed but also provides all facilities and equipment necessary to produce and edit video material. The simulator (below right) is equipped with a high-resolution videocamera attached to a motor-driven sled. The narrow lens of the snorkel requires strong light—four 3000-watt quartz amps. The position of the snorkel in the model is controlled with an additional videocamera (seen at the bottom of the picture). Images are displayed on various video screens and can be mixed and edited during postproduction.

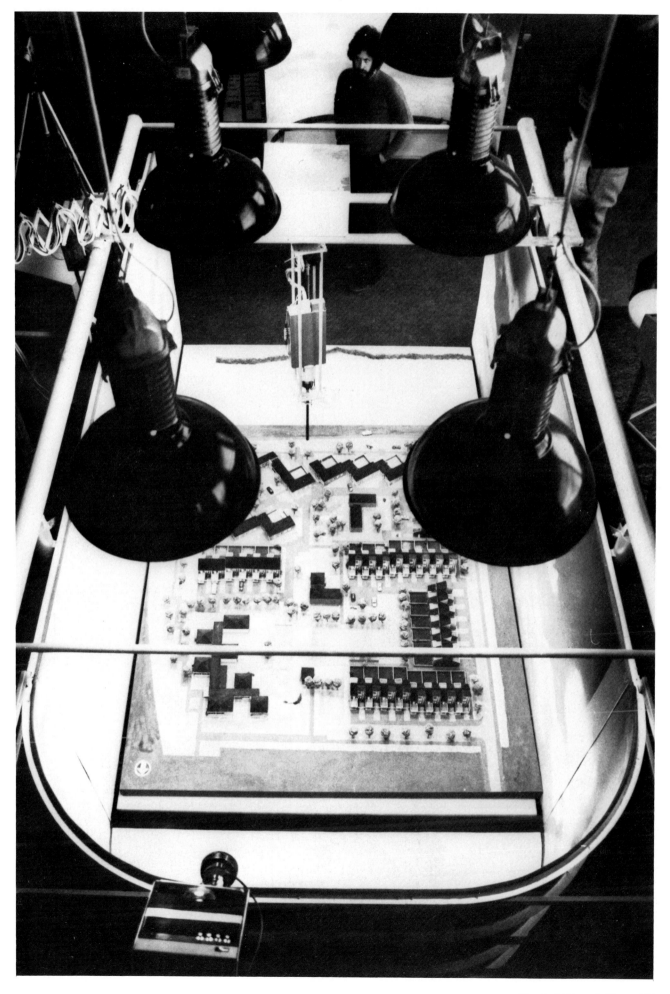

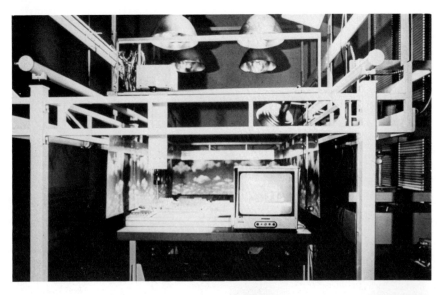

Model Simulators

Another simulator at the university in Delft is relatively complex and requires a trained operator. The system, therefore, is used mainly for research and commercial projects. The camera is driven through the model by setting a certain speed for the stepping motor device.

The direction of movement is controlled by a steering wheel. The location of the snorkel in the model and the actual video image are shown on the video monitor. The background consists of large panels mounted with photographs of clouds.

One of the architectural simulation machines was installed at the School of Architecture and Planning at the University of California in Berkeley. The installation was funded through a large research project to investigate driver's perception when driving through a landscape.

Everything was custom designed for this simulator. Because of the large size of the model, the camera support and lighting had to be specially designed. Because heavy structures generate more vibration than small ones

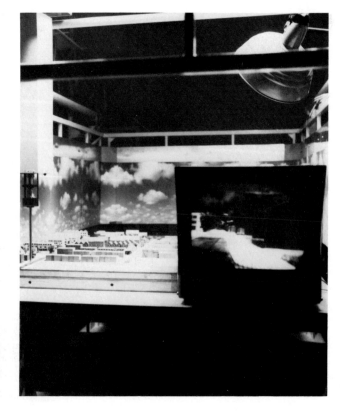

when they are moved, it was not possible to move the snorkel without any vibration over the model.

To provide sharp images, two technologies, video and film, were combined to generate the utmost quality. The camera rig's movements are computer controlled. To select a sequence, the snorkel device is first driven through the model via video-control.

Once the path is defined, a film camera is attached to the snorkel and is moved through the model, taking a sequence of still pictures on 16mm film, running the same path as before the video-controlled test, guided by computer control.

The Berkeley simulator represents the state-of-the-art architectural simulator, topped only by Hollywood's film simulators for trick photography.

Film and video simulators allow architects and planners to visualize designs. This process is based on tedious model building and is very costly if changes are involved. This simulation technique is of extraordinary value if a high-resolution image is required and time to build the model is available. The Berkeley simulator is shown to the right.

Arts & Media Facility

This structure for the M.I.T. campus became the source of a study using the "endoscope" lens attached to a 35mm camera to visualize certain sequences. The design study model used here was an early-phase preliminary design. However, it was a unique design to use in studying views one would expect in walking through the project. A red line was put on the model to indicate the path of the endoscope's photographic sequence. This same technique is the forerunner of many of the more sophisticated computerized movements made today by many simulators.

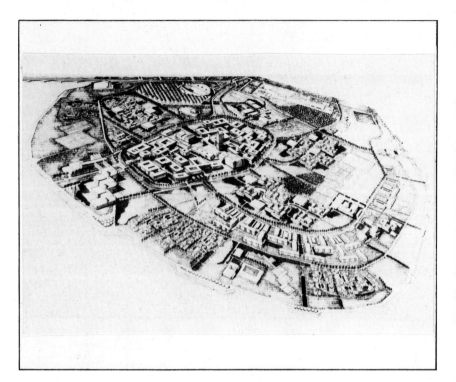

U. of Baghdad Stadium

This master plan was developed for the expansion of Al-Jadriyah Campus to accommodate a total population of 28,000, including students, faculty and their families, and administrative and service staff. Due to the enormous size of the development, it was split into six parcels. The series of model photographs that follow on the next four pages follow that same organization. The largest structures in the expansion program were in the College of Athletics, which featured a major sports arena and stadium to watch swimming events, which became the focal point of the photography. The plan view of the model compares to the hand-drawn plan for the same area. Overall photos were taken on a large-format 4x5 camera with a 90mm wide-angle lens. To achieve maximum depth of field, an aperture opening of f45 was used.

On the edge of the sports complex is the yacht club and two views are shown on the far right; they were taken with a 35mm camera using a 28mm PC (perspective control) lens stopped down to aperture f32.

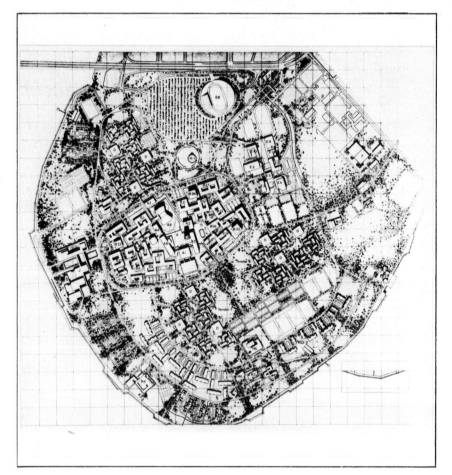

U. of Baghdad Library

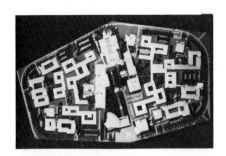

This series shows three different areas, the central and academic buildings (top left), maintenance buildings (top right), and Academy of Fine Arts (bottom). Close-up photos of the central academic cluster were shot with a 28mm PC lens for control of perspective. This features the facility tower. On the far right there is an overall plan view of the maintenance buildings. The pedestrian's view was taken with a special modelscope attachment to a 35mm camera.

The area shown below is the Academy of Fine Arts portion of the model. The plan view was a study model, and the two oblique aerial views show the entry street to the academy complex. They were shot with a 35mm camera with a 150mm lens stopped down to f32.

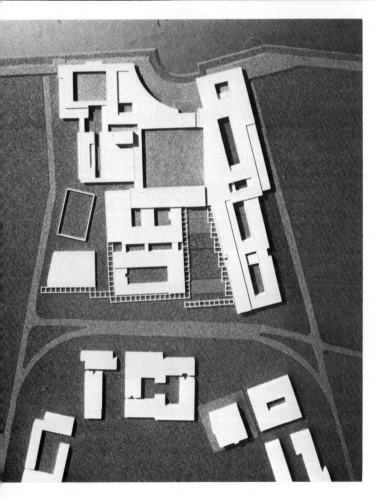

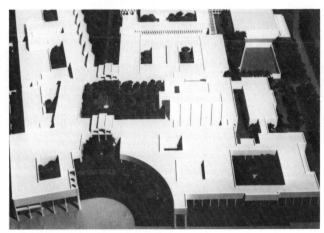

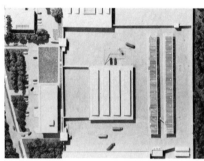

The view on the left, which was taken with a 15mm lens stopped down to aperture f32, shows the building from the river. At this close scale, detail of the small-scale model becomes noticeable.

U. of Baghdad Housing

The housing complex is presented in two different kinds of models: 1:500 and 1:100. The 1:500 model provided the overview of the whole comlex and allowed the visualization of specific arrangements, such as the fountain and pool, through the use of a high-quality modelscope.

Another model in the scale 1:100 was built in sections so one could remove the roof and second floor to study details and to show phasing. At this larger scale, more detailed views are possible. Shade and shadow studies can be made on frontal views, and the camera can be easily lowered to pedestrian level (without having to use a snorkel device). To emphasize the graphical elevation character of the facade shots, a telephoto lens (200mm) was used.

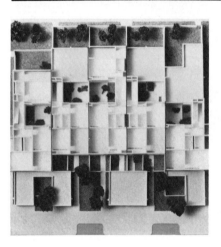

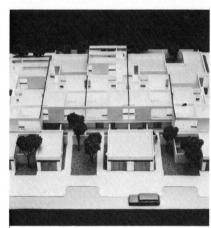

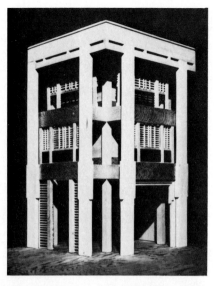

U. of Baghdad Administration

This large-scale partial wooden model was developed to study sunshading designs for the facade of the administration building. There is a combination of images: the typical flat elevation and a frontal oblique. The interior view shows how natural sunlight would enter the space through the louvers. Other parts of the project were studied in more detail using larger-scaled wooden models. The two views on the far right are experimental in nature. In the top right, light is projected from inside the model and special-effects "stars" are created with pinhole spots and star filters. The photo at lower right represents a frog's view of the space. It was created by placing the model on a sheet of glass and putting the camera under the glass aiming upwards.

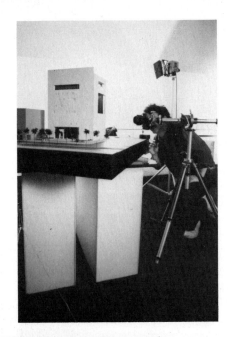

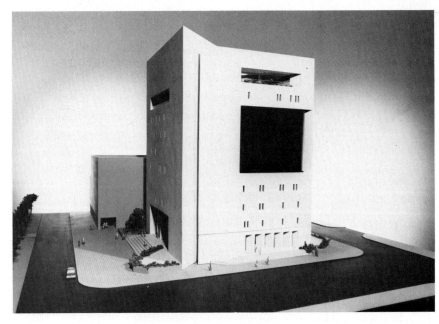

Science Foundation

This model had very sophisticated lights and transformers built into it for special effects, so most of the exposures were time exposures. Different effects of light were studied photographically. Since the building was surrounded by other buildings, the model maker put toned plexiglass on the edge of the plexiglass box of the model so when you view it from outside you can see the outlines of other buildings. The view below shows the pendulum hanging in the vast interior court. The shot was taken with a 15mm wide-angle lens. The others were shot with a 28mm lens with perspective control.

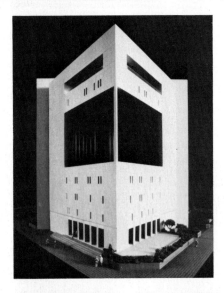

Engineering Models

In today's world of engineering and design, we have all heard of CAD/CAM. Whereas these systems definitely have their places in the world of engineering, there is a nonprofit organization dedicated to the use and promotion of the physical scale model as a design and information tool—the American Engineering Model Society (AEMS).

The AEMS was organized in 1968 and promotes the use of models in industry, science, and government through the exchange of technical information concerning the use of models as design tools.

Conceptual ideas need expansion or refinement to achieve their fullest impact. Models can help by showing the third dimension. In them, we see the reality of spaces in height, depth, and width—the relationship of forms and flow of design.

Models permit fuller communication of the architect's or designer's creative vision. The time usually spent explaining physical components and visual appeal can be spent discussing points often not reviewed when sketches alone are presented.

Communication of design and architectural concepts frequently is directed to a broad spectrum of society, beyond the architects and their clients. Targets include public agencies, financial institutions, business leaders, and industrial firms. Large groups better understand projects by seeing a model. In this day of community action groups and citizen representation, the public wants to know and the model helps them understand.

The "Process Industry," which is chemical, petrochemical, and food, is oriented to the use of models as an engineering tool.

Designing with a model is a matter of thinking in three dimensions and working directly on the model. To best

  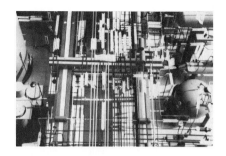

serve this purpose and be of economic value to the complete engineering package, the model is produced without the aid of piping drawings.

A check model identifies interferences, inconsistencies, and omissions on orthographic drawings. It also provides and encourages constructive feedback to coordinate the various facets involved in an engineering package.

Engineers experienced in the use of models are confident that models are far superior to standard orthographic drawings.

During the course of new product development, the engineer arrives at a time when he or she must be absolutely positive that the design will work. This is the time to turn to the engineering prototype model, the ultimate method of simulation. It is the method that most closely duplicates the real article, using the same material, size, and operating principles. Its usage is primarily for technical testing to determine design feasibility and to solidify engineering concepts.

The prototype tends to promote group participation, which is a good way of achieving design coherence and problem awareness.

The prototype model can be the most comforting simulation device to engineering, management, and customer alike because it can establish absolute design credibility.

Engineering Models

A preliminary model is used early in the design study to work out the ideal equipment arrangement. This is a rough model of the structure and equipment that can be changed and studied until a general layout is agreed upon.

Operating personnel can be fully oriented to a new facility or equipment before the facility is placed in operation. This helps to eliminate operational delays and costly errors.

Today's technology has made the problem of communicating design and function to user personnel more difficult. Training models make available a better way of communicating and teaching.

Engineering models have three major uses: for design and design check, as a construction aid, and for operator training. Other uses may include client reviews, procedure analysis and preparation, construction planning and scheduling, safety studies, future maintenance studies, and contract management.

Engineering models are the heart of the design process. The model includes all your disciplines on one drawing. Designers and engineers can explore alternatives faster and select the best one.

Plant Model Photography

The photography of chemical plant models is a specialty that requires expert lighting and photographic skill. Therefore, a 4x5 format is generally best to record the detail. High-resolution film is also necessary in order to record the extreme detail in the depth of the model.

Wonderwall

The Wonderwall is the symbol for the 1984 World's Fair. An architectural focal point, it snakes along the street, close to the fair's entrance.

Conceptually it is novel, designed to boggle the mind and dazzle the eye. Structurally it is simple—2400 feet long, 10 feet thick, and three stories high—containing shops, food stands, stages, video arcades, and rest areas.

Its fairy-tale silhouettes are culled from eighteenth-century Italian drawings, Greek temples, medieval castles, art deco ornamentation, and Gothic architectural details. Some sections are direct descendants of other buildings, such as the aviary in the Borghese Gardens in Rome, or the Palace of Fine Arts built for the 1915 San Francisco World's Fair.

Structurally, the Wonderwall is deceptively simple; it is put together like a jigsaw puzzle. The base supports scaffolding that secures decorative metal flats rising as high as 40 feet. The flats are like theater scenery.

Phased Development

Vertical expansion is a solution this firm has used successfully for a number of clients faced with a tighter marketplace. It is a method of designing buildings, or of adding onto existing ones, that responds financially and architecturally to the realities of the economy.

In designing vertical expansion projects, provisions must be made for strengthened foundations and structure, for a mechanical system that can be built in increments, for practical elevatoring, and for construction staging for the later phases. It also means making design decisions re-

garding the building's appearance that are appropriate at either a larger or smaller scale.

The challenge of designing a vertical expansion project is to make the building look good at any size, tall or short. If the building never grows any taller, which could happen if economic conditions do not warrant expansion, the small tower must appear finished in all its details. If the building does expand, the upper and lower portions of the building must form a unified whole, with the proportions of both sections in harmony with each other and appropriate to the full-sized building.

First United Methodist

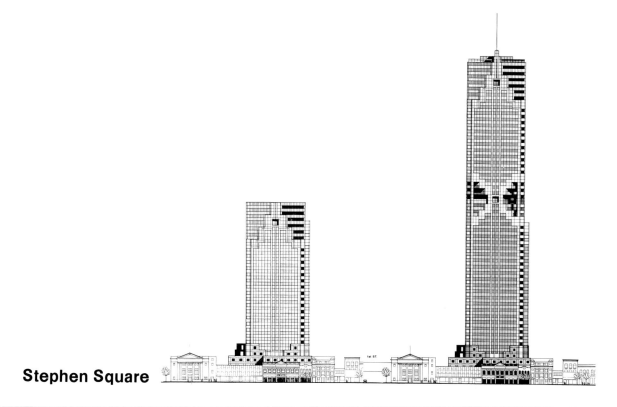

Stephen Square

Photomontages

Camera positions chosen for photomontages should represent the most prominent public vantage points, and the choice of camera format and lenses should simulate the perception of the human eye. Further, the subject's lighting and texture should highlight the designer's objectives.

The lenses used, for both the site and model photography, were 35mm and 28mm PC (perspective control) lenses. Important issues in this assignment were the appearance and visibility of a historic building behind the proposed one and the casting of as little shadow as possible onto Union Square (right).

Architectural photomontages require the orchestrated skills of an urban designer's and photographer's eyes, an architect's sense of perspective, and—last, but by no means least—the cooperation of a master photographic printer. Not surprisingly, every interest appears to benefit in the process: a grateful citizenry, the city planning staff, environmental consultants, architects, and the developer, proudly showing off (and marketing) a worthy project.

580 California Street

212 Stockton Street

Park Avenue Synagogue

In portraying this addition to an existing synagogue, the architects chose to use model photography to help visualize the three-dimensional nature of the design. The suspension members shown at the corner of the structure are pipe columns, fireproofed and sheathed in bronze. The rest of the facade is clear glass. In addition, they used the model photo set into a photograph of the actual site in a photomontage, which adds more depth and realism than the straight-on viewpoint.

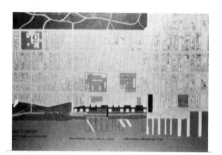

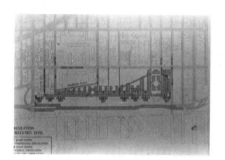
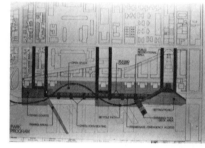

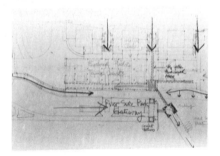

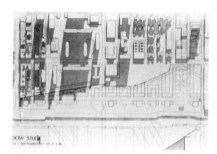
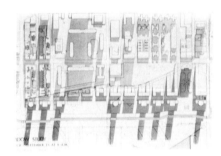

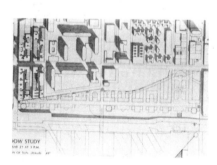

Lincoln West

This project was planned for one of the largest remaining parcels of land in Manhattan, over the old Penn Central yards, which were to remain active in the final scheme. A project of this size requires a lot of visual tools to help explain it to city officials and the community. Aerial photos of the site were combined with corresponding aerial views of the model. Plan views of the model were coordinated with rendered site plans and photographed in the same size and framing. Many other visuals were created in plan view to explain traffic patterns, access to the site, view corridors, and density patterns. Sketch plans, showing details and access to the public park, were combined with quick sketches showing scenes from a pedestrian's viewpoint. Shadow studies in plan view were prepared showing both the before and after conditions of morning and afternoon shadows cast from the project's building onto the surrounding areas.

A mass model without detail was built of the project and photographed from many angles. One of those views was from across the Hudson River and portrayed the new structure in relation to the existing skyline. Sketches supplemented the model photographs and concentrated on portraying the environmental quality of the proposed development.

Tehran Airport

The concept behind this international airport's basic design was its role as a single transportation complex. The linear development of the spine linking Tehran and the terminal allows passengers to travel in express rail transit from the city to the airport.

Terminal areas were arranged in double modules along the spine. To describe the terminal configurations and functions, an elaborate "take-apart" model was constructed wherein each floor level could be studied in detail.

Plans were drawn of each corresponding level to the model. The presentation material also included interior renderings to complement the model photos. The model was built with a concealed lighting system, which lit up not only the structures but the runways as well.

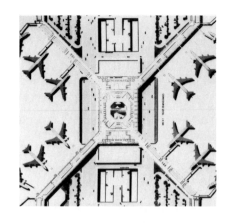

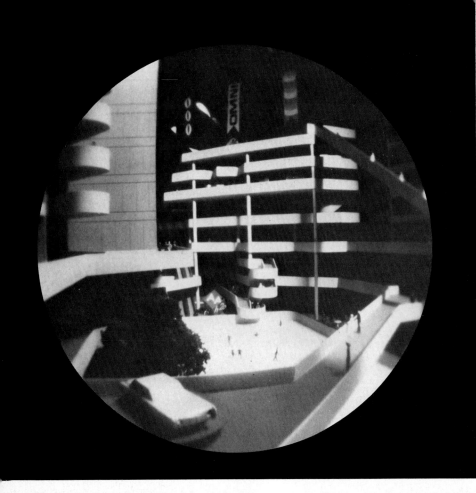

Omni

This model was used to promote public relations and pre-leasing. It was primarily constructed of plastics—plexiglass and styrene. Of special interest are the lower levels of the model, which include interior details that can be viewed through clear glass, and fiber optic lighting, which illuminates the interiors. The circular photographs were taken through a modelscope.

Norfolk Gardens

Used as a public relations promotion this model, constructed of plastics, highlights this predominantly bronze plexiglass exterior, which is highly detailed. The circular photograph taken through a modelscope gives a unique view of the fiber-optically illuminated interiors.

Peachtree Summit

Constructed of plastics, plexiglass, and styrene, this model was an early preliminary design for study and presentation. The circular photograph, taken through a modelscope, shows a view of an indoor ice rink.

Mercantile Center

Highly detailed, this model was constructed of plastics. Details include the injection-molded trusses and columns, fiber optics, and animated lighting. It was used for a preliminary study and for presentation.

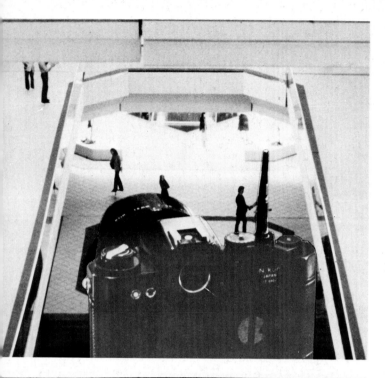

Copley Place

The model was constructed in such a way that it could be taken apart and the camera placed inside it. These sequences actually simulate the walk through the shopping mall. The choice of lens is critical in this type of model photography so that the distortion is kept at a minimum. This has to be figured in relation to the scale of the model.

Scale people are included in this model to give it life and a sense of movement and activity. They were photographed in scale, on instant color print film and then cut out and placed within the model. If a pin is glued to the cutout figure, it can be moved around as the camera angle changes.

The camera should be equipped with a ground glass that has a horizontal and vertical grid etched into it. This allows the photographer to control the perspective distortion and to avoid barrel distortion by previewing in the ground glass any views that might produce distortion. Perspective control lenses are not as useful in this kind of model photography since there is much less room to move around.

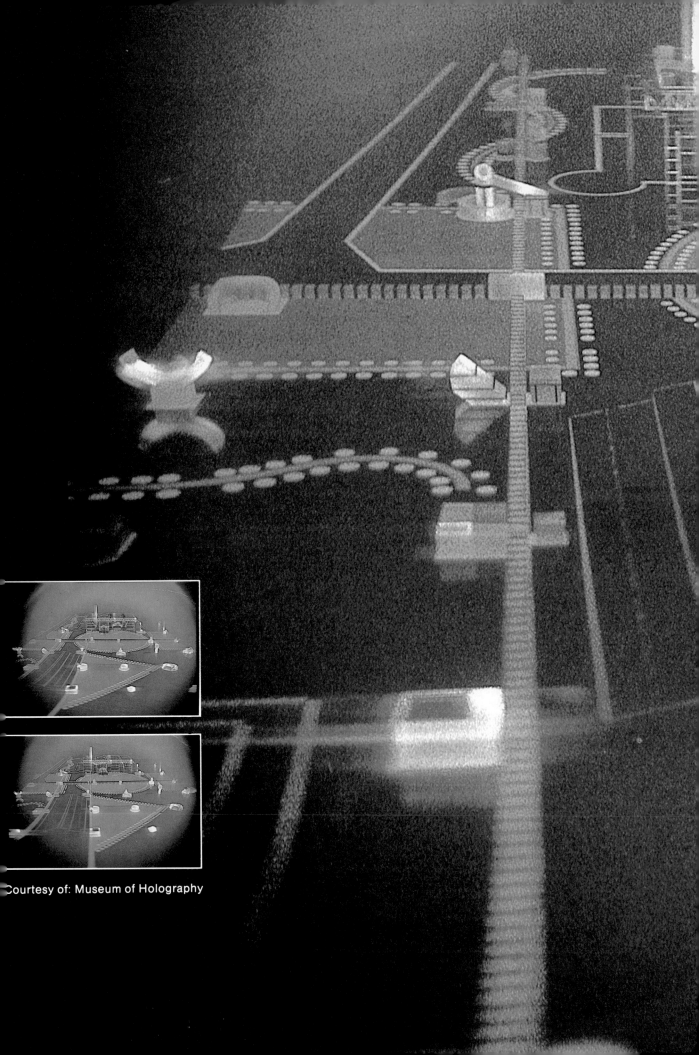

Courtesy of: Museum of Holography

Spivok Residence

"No square corners" was the directive issued by the client who commissioned the design for the Marin County, California, residence shown here in clay model and contour-map form. Since the 11,000-square-foot structure was to be completely curvilinear, its design created some unusual problems. Prior to awarding this design commission, the client recorded a long list of suggestions in his computer as a guide. Later, after an extensive series of schematic and preliminary design concepts were developed by the firm, design preference evolved into a non-geometric, free-flowing environmental sculpture. Because it was nearly impossible to draw the design concept by traditional means, the building shapes were conceived and sculptured in clay on top of a quarter-inch scale print of the finalized floor plan. Once the sculpture/model was completed for the exterior, a hollow fiberglass casing was made and the interior was sculpted inside the shell.

Drawing the floor plan was a traditional architectural pro-

cess, but traditional elevations and sections were deemed to be too time-consuming and therefore inappropriate for this project. Realizing the difficulty in working from only a floor plan and model to generate information for the computer drafting process, the designers sought out a system that could provide contoured drawings of the exterior and interior surfaces of the model.

Using the services of an aerial photography and mapping firm accurate data was provided that would be digitized for computer display and contour compilations. A precision camera was used to photograph the model, and was shifted for a second photograph to obtain stereoscopic coverage. The drawings are a true technical record of the exterior and interior, void of preconceptions of the design. The system expresses architectural shapes by means of contours, just as a contour map does. For the stereo-compilation of contour maps of the architectural model, a precision stereo-plotting instrument was employed, together with digitizing equipment.

The optical measurement process involved three phases: taking the photographs, digitizing them, and

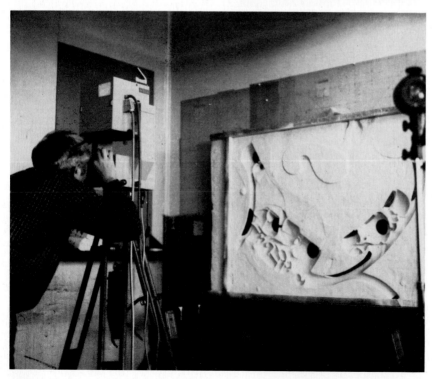

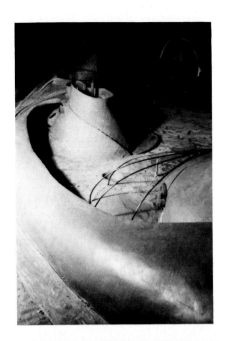

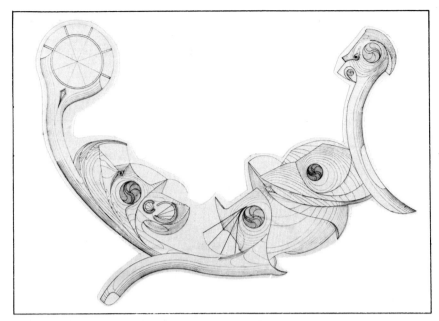

creating a complete display and record of the results. The production of the stereo photographs is the heart of the process.

The universal metric camera used was especially designed for this type of application, but the photographs were created using standard techniques. This process is known as close-range photogrammetry. HLW has applied similar "non-contact" measuring techniques to several other projects including mining, bridge design, and archeology.

The advantages of architectural stereophotogrammetry as an aid in the preparation of plans have yet to be fully exploited. For example, it could be a valuable aid in the study of integration of new structures into existing urban settings.

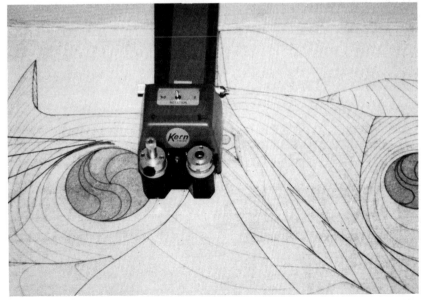

3-D Model Visualization

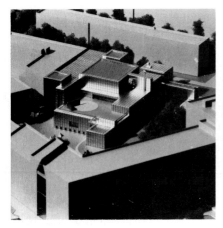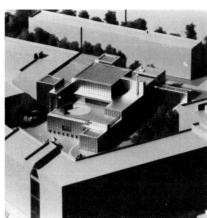

Architectural scale models represent three-dimensional simulations of exterior and interior architectural environments. In contrast to flat graphic media, such as plans, elevation drawings and perspective renderings, physical models allow the spatial perception of three dimensions from any viewpoint.

This depth perception, called stereopsis, is based on the fact that we look at a situation with two eyes, which have a pupillary distance of 65mm for men and 63mm for women. The two different impressions on the retina of each eye are united in one single image in the brain.

The photographic documentation of any architectural scale mode, reproduced as slide or photographic print, always results in a flat, two-dimensional representation of a three-dimensional arrangement. More realistic three-dimensional documentation can only be achieved by simulating the stereoscopic viewing process. Therefore models have to be photographed as image pairs, each representing a view from a slightly different viewing position. Both positions simulate the pupillary distance and will vary depending on the scale of the model and technical specifications of the photographic equipment.

While the "real world" stereopsis is based on an average focal length of 55mm with a pupillary distance (or stereo base) of 60—63mm, stereoscopic model photography requires different settings.

Once the model is set up and the lighting is arranged, stereo pairs can be taken in succession from two different positions, located at a certain distance from each other. This depends on the size and scale of the model, focal length of the lens, and camera format.

Technically one can choose between two methods to achieve a stereo pair. One is to move the model slightly and keep the camera stationary; or move the camera only.

Stereo pairs can be viewed as slides in common "binocular" slide viewers. They can be projected using polarized filters over the lenses which match polarized glasses.

The stereoscopic model photographs shown were taken with wide angle lenses, using the technique of moving the camera laterally for each view. The overall view of the sport facilities of the Bagdhad campus (top) was generated with a stereo base of 4mm. The close-up shot of the piping arrangement (opposite) was done with a stereo base of 2mm as a result of the very short distance to the closest objects and the use of an extreme wide angle lens (15mm).

Stereoscopic presentations of computer graphics displays are produced very similarly to stereoscopic model photographs. Instead of moving the camera or the model, two different views are generated with the computer. Each view is oriented to the same focal point, only shifted by the distance of the stereo base. Images are then computed and displayed on the screen. For display, they can be photographed off the screen and viewed as slides or photographic prints, using the appropriate stereo glasses.

The computer graphics stereo display of a hospital complex (bottom) was generated with a stereoscopic base of two feet, taking into consideration a simulated long focal length and the limited resolution resulting caused by the graphics display unit.

Another option is the direct stereoscopic video display. The video monitor can simultaneously display the left and right eye images. Electro-optical shuttering glasses are used in conjunction with a stereo display for viewing, providing a flicker-free, full color, three-dimensional display. This display technology has improved recently and might have substantial impact on computer graphics-based display systems where true three-dimensional displays are of great importance.

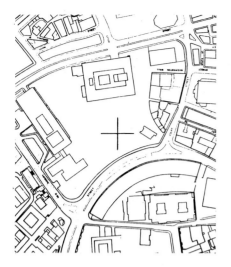

Panorama Photography

Usually the architectural photographer takes a "window" out of the 360° panorama, isolating it from its surroundings. That window depends on the angle of view of the lens and the distance from the subject. He or she composes that particular window very carefully because it is the replication of the scene chosen in the camera. In some cases it is helpful to see how an architectural pro-

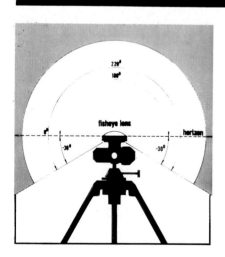

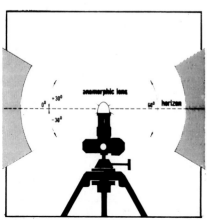

Two other techniques used to shoot panoramas are the fisheye lens and the anamorphic lens. Both optical systems give a circular image and shoot a 360° panorama, but they are completely different in the way they do it.

The fisheye lens shoots a sphere, a kind of a bubble around the lens, and this bubble is a half-sphere. The center of this sphere is always the film plane. The fisheye lens allows us to shoot the 360° panorama where the viewer is in the center and the surrounding environment is pictured on the film plane as a two-dimensional image that presents a projected sphere.

The other technique, to shoot a panorama with the anamorphic lens, is very much different from the fisheye technique. Whereas with the fisheye technique you have the total bubble, the whole sphere over the camera, the anamorphic lens selects only a spherical zone around the lens. The zone around the lens is 30° from the horizontal film plane if the camera is positioned vertically with the film plane horizontal or parallel to the ground.

The perspective distortion of this lens is much less than that of the fisheye lens. On one image the buildings go to the center (fisheye) and on the other, the buildings go out of the center (anamorphic).

124

ject relates to its total 360°
environment.

The first technique uses a
new development of an old
camera, which was introduced
at the end of the nineteenth
century to photograph panoramic scenes. Some of these
are still in use today. Today,
there is also a 35mm camera
that produces panoramas by
exposing the film through a slit
as the camera rotates 360°
around the center axis.

This camera is spring driven
and is not limited to one 360°
picture per roll of film. Neither
does it limit where the panorama begins or ends.

This is a relatively easy way
to get seamless panoramas
without a great deal of money,
technical background, or sophisticated laboratory equipment to achieve results. The
overall effect is far more re-
vealing and impressive than a
single picture.

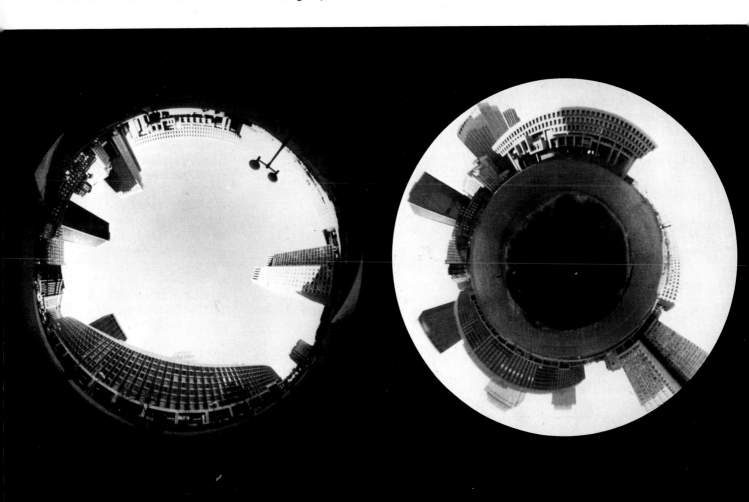

North River

This presentation was made to the New York City Art Commission to assure that the plant design was harmonious with the long-term aesthetic interest of the city. The architectural theme of arches is compatible with the surrounding historic environment in the area as well as with the arched structures on nearby bridge and viaduct supports. To demonstrate this, the architects went to the site and took a series of panoramic photos, placing the site in the middle of the three-panel sequence. A drawing was made to the same scale as the panoramas and superimposed onto the photographs. The entire panel was then colored for the presentation. A scaled mock-up of the precast concrete panels was made to study the effect of sunlight and shadow on the textured surface. A sample of a completed panel can be compared to the mock-up.

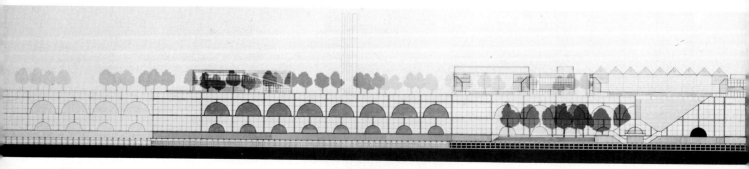

Mediatecture

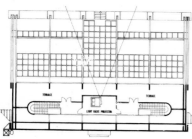

This project was an entry for a design competition titled "A House for Karl Friedrich Schinkel." The entry not only used computer graphics as a visualization tool but conceptualized various applications of this technology into the design itself.

How Schinkel would live if he lived today and the most appropriate surroundings for his professional activities were projected. As one of the most famous architects of the classic epoch of European architecture, Schinkel generated numerous alternatives for a specific design project, very often including sketches presenting different styles. Schinkel was also involved in the design of stage sets for the Berlin Opera House. Taking these as a base for his projected activities in the twentieth century, the competition entry located him in Los Angeles, close to the film industry of Hollywood and the computer industry of Silicon Valley. He has his private computer-graphics-supported design studio in the triangular room on the second floor of the main building. Designs are projected in real scale on a large, private screen, located behind the pool at the north wall of the estate.

(cont'd on Pg. 130)

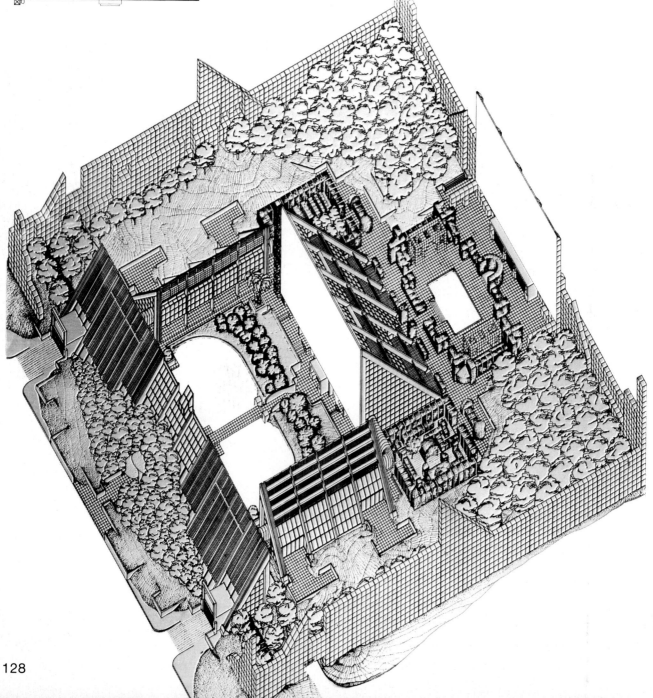

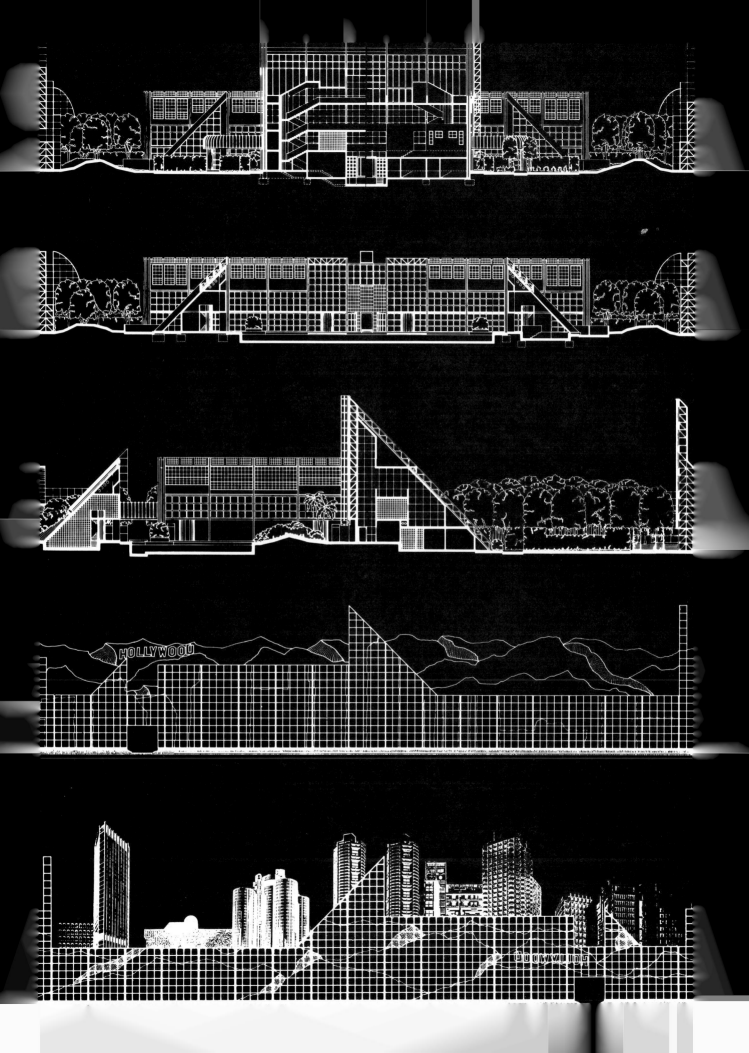

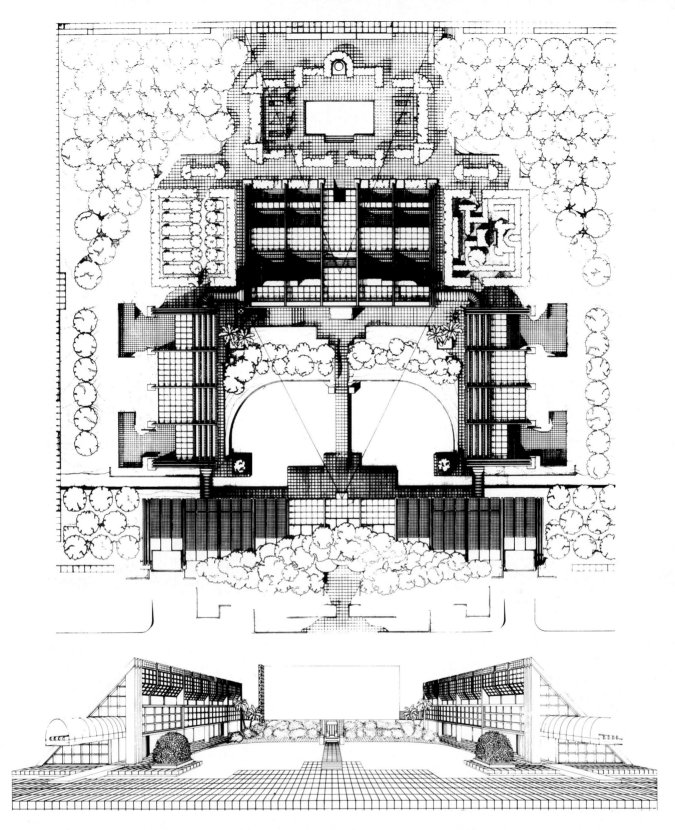

The house facade presents the "public" facade. It is a large screen, the size of a drive-in movie screen, symbolizing one of the most genuine artifacts of this region. This screen fulfills the function of a projection surface for video, computer graphics, and laser projections after sunset. For daytime display, computer-generated images are plotted with a large ink-jet plotter over the whole area of the public facade. The people who pass by are not looking at a permanent image like a built facade. Commuters witness a daily change of plotted images which are not limited to architectural messages but can include imagery or poetry. During the evenings they can participate in Schinkel's design exercises or witness displays of avant-garde computer graphics displays.

The complex itself is equipped with high-tech building elements. Ultrasonic sensors, directed to the public streets, detect movements and transfer them, through a computer program, into visual displays on the facade during night hours.

MULTI-FUNCTIONAL MEDIA SCREEN FOR DISPLAY OF:

BAROQUE

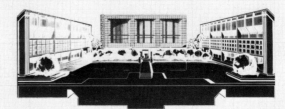

POST MODERN

INTERNATIONAL STYLE

ARCHITECTURAL
FACADES

INDUSTRIAL

ARCHITECTURAL
SECTIONS

INDUSTRIAL

RESIDENTIAL

IMAGES

NON-ARCHITECTURAL
MESSAGES

TEXT

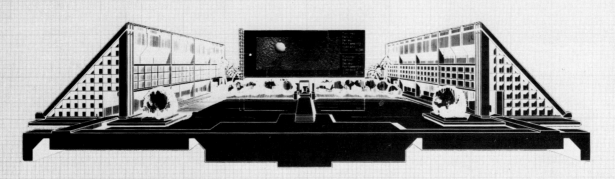

LIVE PROJECTION OF COMPUTER-GENERATED IMAGES

3-D Visualization

There are some techniques for visualizing projects that may sound exotic but in reality are quite simple. If the technology were more readily available, more people would experiment with these techniques. The first is the use of lenticular photography to illustrate phases of a design without moving models around.

By simply tilting the photograph, you can observe the different phases illustrated by the lenticular plate. This is accomplished by taking exact registration photos of a model and transferring the exposures onto a lenticular film with a lenticular screen. The sandwiched film is what causes the picture to change as you tilt the plate, similar to traditional three-dimensional postcards.

Two techniques that accomplish simulation of a building in its actual site are quite opposite in preparation—one is technically very easy, the other is rather difficult. On the top right is an illustration of how a hologram, which was produced from a model of a building, could later be viewed superimposed over its intended future site.

In order to photograph an "unphotographable image" the sunlight had to strike the holographic plate in just the right way and time of day. You

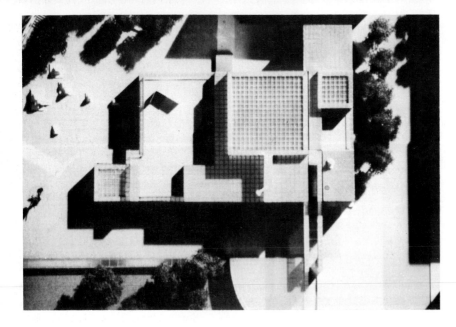

could then see the holo-
graphic image floating above
the site. This image was photographed using a 15mm wide-
angle lens, which captured the
image of the building as projected by a holographic image
floating over the site.

Another technique involving
far less sophisticated technology than holographic
images is the one seen at the
bottom right. A picture of the
model is taken with an endoscope camera to position the
viewer at pedestrian level
scaled to the small model. A
Cibachrome color print is
made directly from the slide
that results, and the building
shape is cut out and held up in
front of the site in position, as
if it's located on the site. A
photograph is then taken
using a 15mm lens, of the
building positioned into the
actual site.

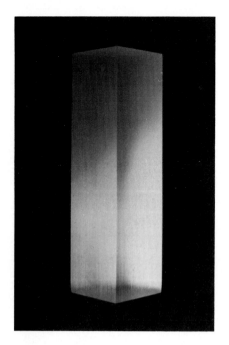
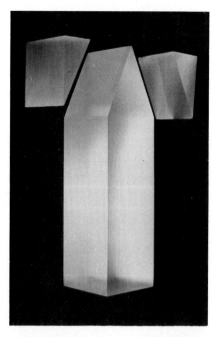

Fountain Place

Exacting attention to perspective and size are critical to achieving an accurate photocomposite.

A detailed area map was used to calculate exact distance between the site within the city and the distance from that site while photographing the skyline. This measurement made it possible to establish the ratio between this distance and the actual height of the proposed building. The same height/distance ratio was applied to the model height to determine the distance from which to photograph it. The angle was based on the city map, and the model was positioned to match the angle of the city photo. The two accurately aligned and sized photos were then retouched to create an 8x10 transparency.

In order to show how the unique faceted design was derived from a simple geometric shape, a rectangular plexiglass mass was shown. Then, sections were removed, as if carved away at a 60° angle. Colored lighting was used to add aesthetic appeal. The variations of the shape were shown by rotating the prism-like shape through five views.

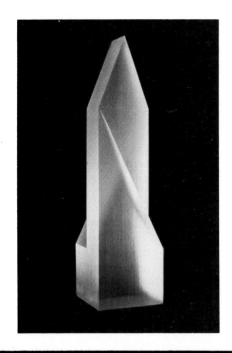

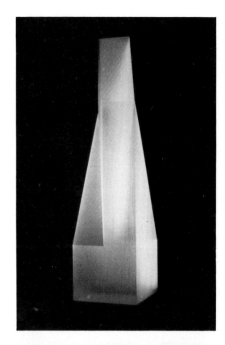

Fujiya Sign

The world's first fiber optic projection system is located on the busiest corner of one of the busiest areas in all the world: The Ginza in Tokyo.

Here's a technology that has been scientifically demonstrated for over a century but, except for some limited applications, has been all but overlooked by the sign industry.

Now, slides, animation, movies, and weather information can all be shown to thousands of daily passersby on Fujiya's 7-meter-high, 10-meter-wide oval screen. The sign becomes more than advertising; it potentially becomes an information center similar to several of those landmarks on several other corners of the world: Times Square and Picadilly Circus.

Fujiya could use the same film that they now use for television commercials. They could use the same budget they have for their advertising on film and put it toward advertising with fiber optics.

An earlier design proposal, which suggested using argon and krypton lasers, would have provided extra brightness, but several factors labeled the laser inappropriate.

The laser's capabilities, though perhaps providing a brighter light, are limited to line drawings; a fiber optic system, however, can "fill in" those line drawings and provide the equivalent of halftone printing.

The entire system, at present, can accommodate 192 slides projected by the "dissolving method." Slide projection is accomplished by a remote control system designed so that the slide sequence can be changed at any time.

The Fujiya 7-by-10-meter oval screen with its corporate Spencerian "F" trademark with daisy contains 56,000 2-mm diameter optical fibers. Each fiber is placed on a surface 3 cm apart on center each way and protruding slightly in front of the F mark. During the day, the mirror-finished, stainless steel trademark is visible. At night, however, the trademark is obliterated; it's now the animation's time to "shine."

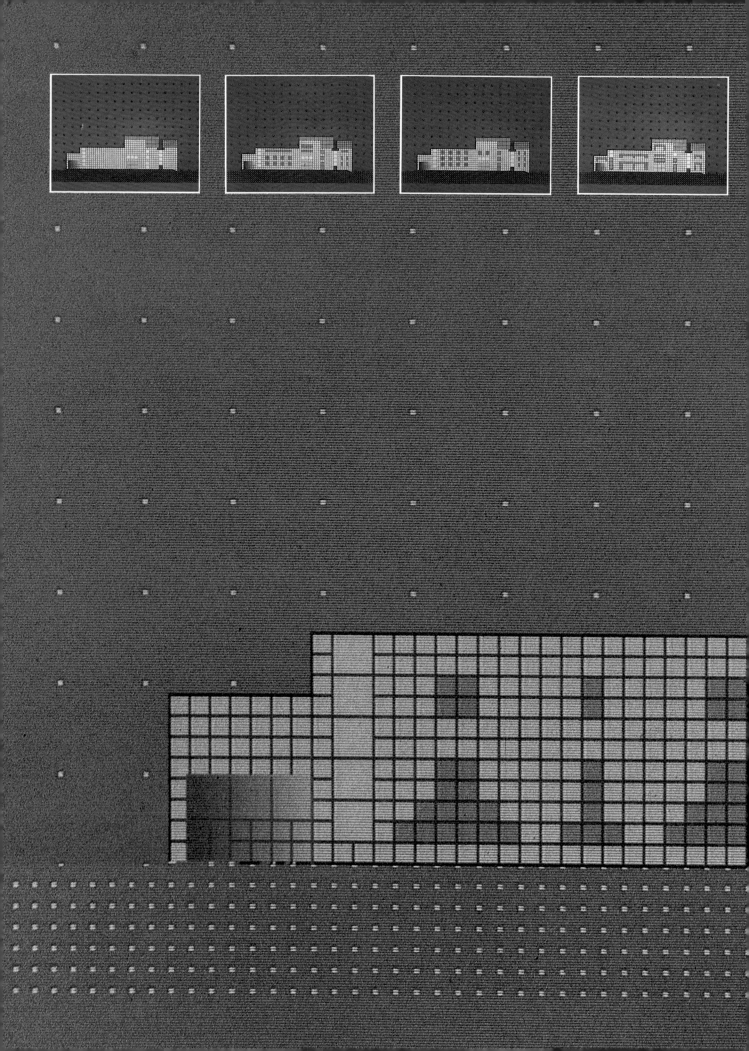

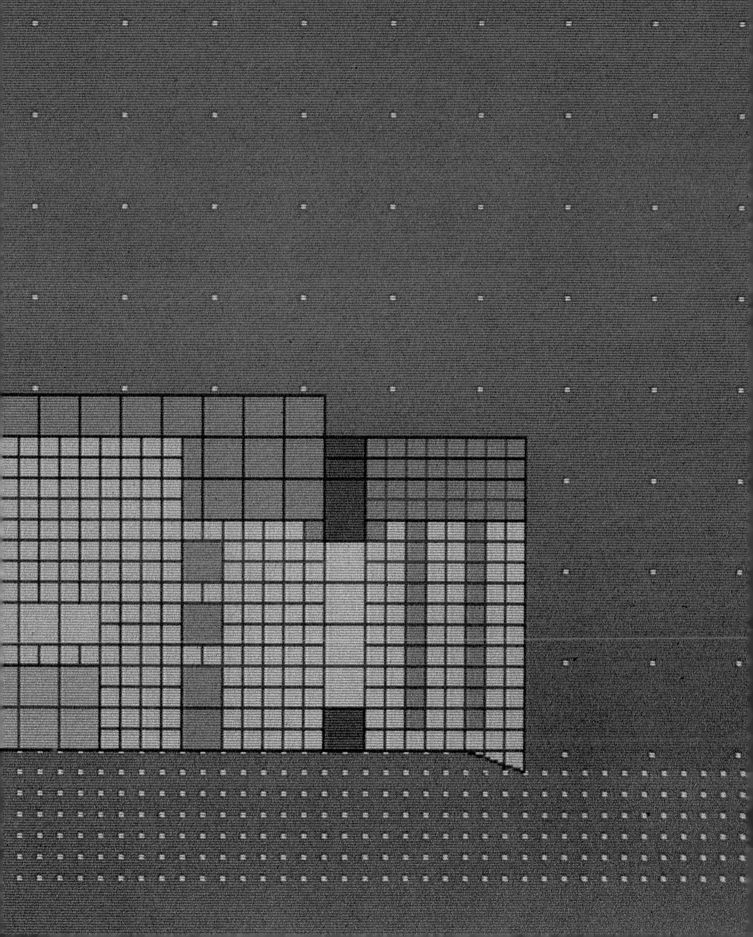

Computer Sketches

These computer graphics sketches were not generated on an architectural design project but were developed for experiments of architectural visualization. In the very early design stage, architects use various means to communicate a design to a client. It is not unusual for first sketches to be produced in restaurants on napkins and with felt tip pens.

Here a painting program was developed for a raster scan computer graphics system which allows the user to draw dots with different diameters. By moving the stylus over the digitizing tablet, you generate a sequence of dots following a line pattern, which produces very diffused lines. The effect is a little bit like running a felt pen over a napkin.

There is a choice of 256 colors that can be combined and displayed on the screen for a total of 4.5 million color combinations, so a palette is virtually unlimited. You can use this system not only to draw lines, but also to color areas. You can define certain parts of the building with color to enhance the resolution step-by-step.

The illustration shows the rough notation of outlines of the elements. With an electronic brush, you can draw while the width and density of the line are controlled by computer.

The picture above shows the coloring surfaces. When the lines fill the rectangle, it becomes a border. You can flood this bordered area and generate a colored surface. You can also make handwritten notations or marks for the design with the same stylus in the same way you draw lines. You can do handwritten text, or if you prefer, typewritten text. Further enhancements allow you to change colors. You can generate very abstract architectural forms to visualize your idea.

The organic forms of this napkin-sketch visualization, of course, can be straightened out and can be changed into geometric shapes. These geometric forms are generated with a line program and fill-in patterns. They are used to fill surfaces, to copy programs, to repeat lines, and to generate squares for windows and doors.

The experiments here are based on the architect's design of the Arts and Media Facilities Building, although these variations and experiments bear no relation to the design decisions. Here, a video digitizing camera was used to scan line drawings. The line drawing shows different kinds of patterns and a facade. Both were then included in the computer memory after they were digitized. With the computer program, certain elements of the center row are selected and placed on the facade.

The original design functioned as a base. Using a computer program, outlines and shapes were entered. Then, using the painting program, different window positions and window layouts were placed on the facade. This allowed the generation of many variations with the help of a flat-field camera. Each variation was photographed on slide material and could then be evaluated during an optimization process.

The computer also allows change of colors and backgrounds. When going from architectural presentation to graphic presentations, you can produce any different color scheme and combination.

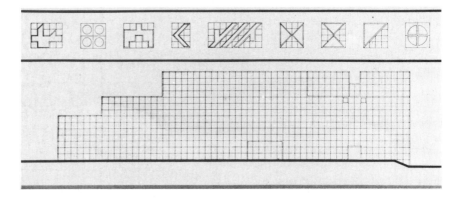

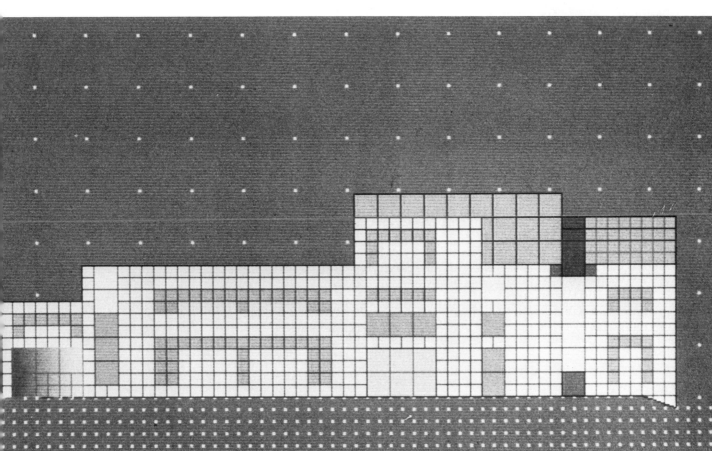

Alamo Square

Here is an application of optical digitizing in combination with a computer graphics painting program. The objective was to digitize drawings, which were generated with manual drafting, and color code them with the computer as you would normally do with markers or color pens. The difference is that you can not only color them, but can also move certain elements as was shown previously with the primitive napkin-sketch principle.

The drawing of a street elevation produced a very abstract design which was then digitized with a video camera and entered into the computer memory. The facade was copied two times with the computer. Certain small particles were moved and colors were changed so the variations of the facade became visible.

The picture on the bottom is a detail shot which shows the pixelization of the picture surfaces. With this method, the computer can be used to generate visual material quickly and accurately. The electronic paint program generates variations and alternatives much faster and more efficiently than can be done with traditional tools.

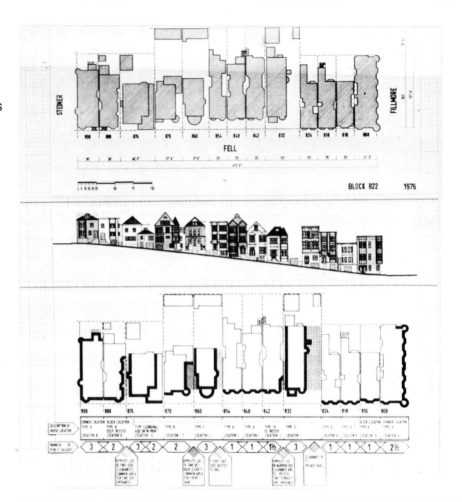

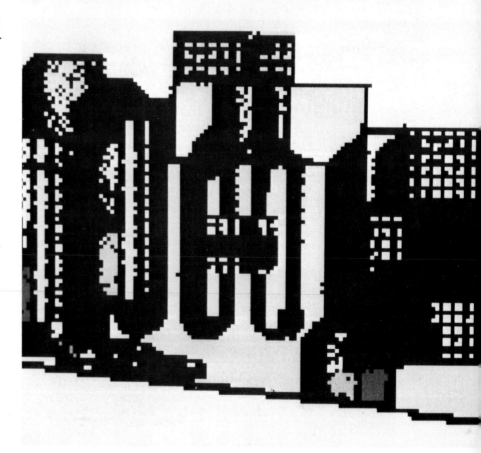

142

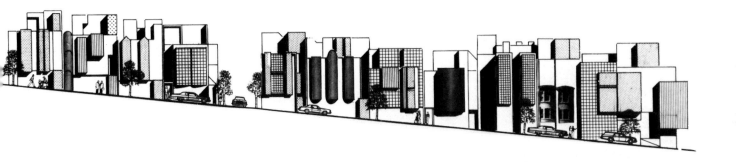

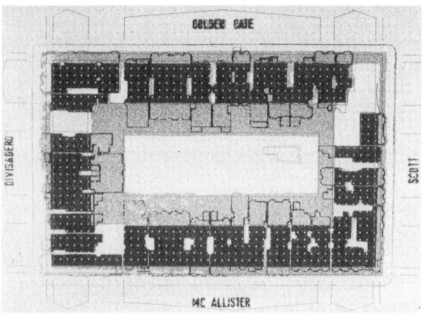

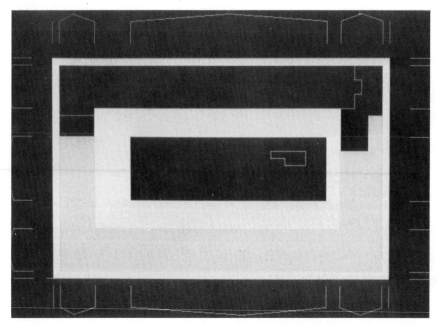

"N" Plan

This program was the major part of a research project. The principal idea was to use the computer as architects use tracing paper—to design using overlays and to quantify certain areas. You begin with a line drawing generated manually.

This drawing is then optically digitized with a video camera and entered into the memory of the computer. The different bit planes of the computer are then separated into layers that contain the digitized images. In this case, three planes were used so there were five planes left for the computer graphics to be used as overlays. You can then draw over the displayed digitized image while you are observing it.

The three-bit image appeared on the screen. The next image gives an idea of how lines can be laid over an existing drawing, relating to a certain grid. This grid had to be generated according to the scale of the drawing on the screen. There is a scale line on the top so the grid was in an appropriate scale. You can stretch lines and draw lines from grid point to grid point. Certain borders, zones, and built elements were defined.

The flooding program of the computer allowed these areas to flood, but you always have transparency where you can actually see through the colored computer graphics surface to the actual distribution of the buildings.

The computer graphics program allows you to scan the areas and take the number of pixels multiplied by a certain factor to give you an approximation of the number of square feet in certain zones.

The data, which is entered here automatically, can be extruded in its height as an axonometric. The number of pixels it is shifted is in relation to the height and the scale of the display. That's a very easy way which avoids heavy computation, while in the photo-perspective display, you have

144

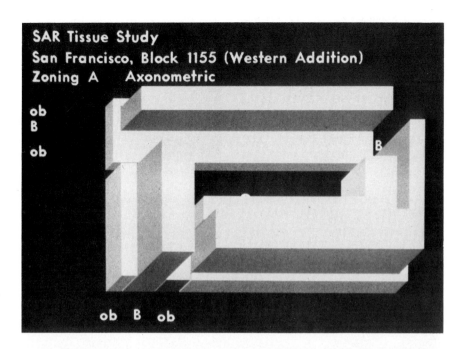

SAR Tissue Study
San Francisco, Block 1155 (Western Addition)
Zoning A   Axonometric

ob
B
ob

B

ob B ob

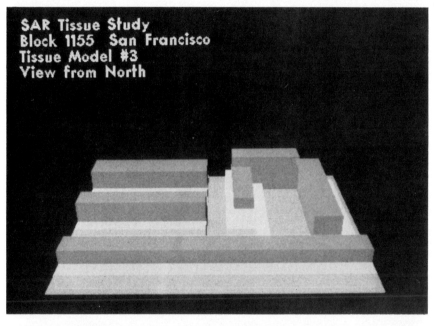

SAR Tissue Study
Block 1155 San Francisco
Tissue Model #3
View from North

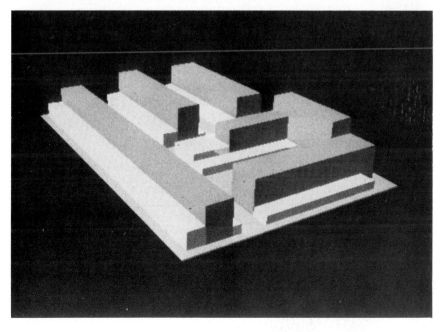

a normal perspective program. You cannot, in this case, retrieve data that is entered in two dimensions for the perspective.

In addition to generating a database for an axonometric, you can also generate a database for real three-dimensional perspectives. From the three-dimensional you can generate perspectives from any distance or view angle.

Computer Wall Painting

Architects work in three dimensions. In general they draw a plan or draw a perspective and finally build a model and photograph it. The computer allows you to generate, from the very beginning, a three-dimensional database with not only the thickness of material but the extension in three dimensions.

Just as you would build a model with little blocks, you're able to build with electronic volumes. This example shows the comparison of a rough working model and the equivalent electronic model.

This was in a very early stage of three-dimensional visualization, but it shows that any shapes you can present with a working model can also be presented by computer.

A comparison is shown of a working model and an electronic model on a CRT using the three-dimensional database.

On the right is a device developed at M.I.T.'s Visual Language Workshop. It is a large-scale plotter, which allows a plot using a spray-painting method on large surfaces, a plot of colored computer data. This could become a major influence on certain architectural simulations. With a large-scale plotter it would be possible to generate the facade on a computer and previsualize it in full scale before it is built.

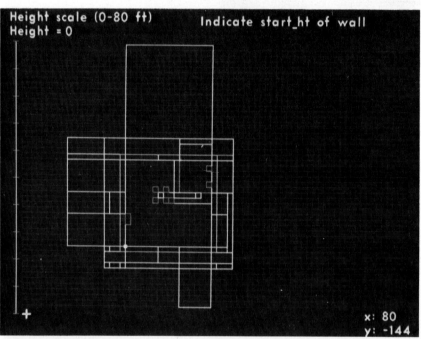

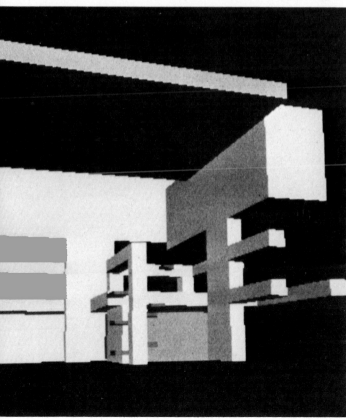

Painter Hill House

This residential design was computerized, after it had been manually drawn up, to study further applications of the computer painting program. The site plan was digitized and overlaid with computer graphics. The landscaping and pond were added. Floor plans were generated. The walls were given height and shadows by shifting the pixels. An axonometric was generated by copying pixel displays diagonally. The painted elevations were produced by filling in the straight line areas with color. An additional database was generated to produce a perspective view. The dots in the front and back are not part of the database; they were used to enhance the graphic appearance of the image.

The section shows the winter and summer angles of the sun, but, more important, it

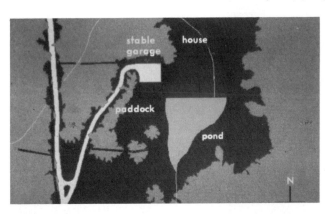

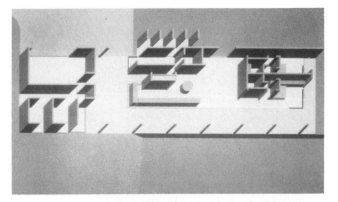

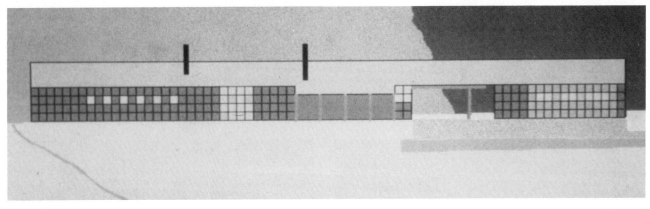

shows a person generated
through optical digitization
and picture-mapped into the
computer graphics. The detail
on the right shows the resolution of this "person." You can
actually enhance a computer-
generated drawing by com-
bining photographic images,
which can be inserted into the
computer graphics.

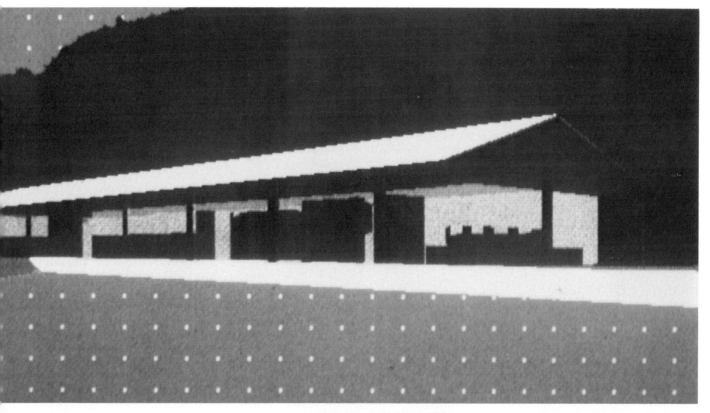

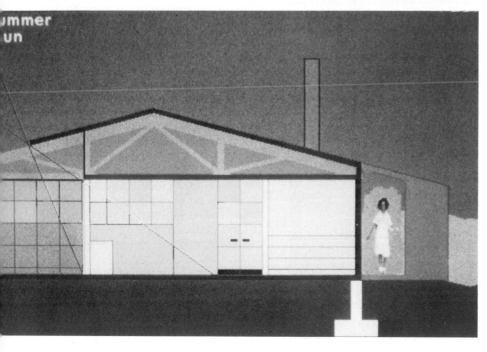

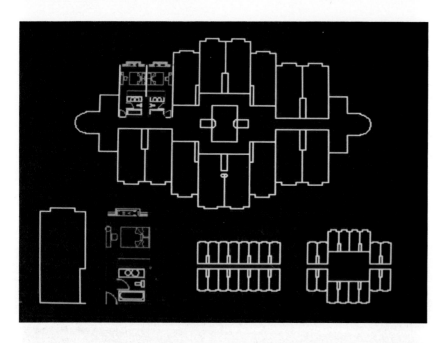

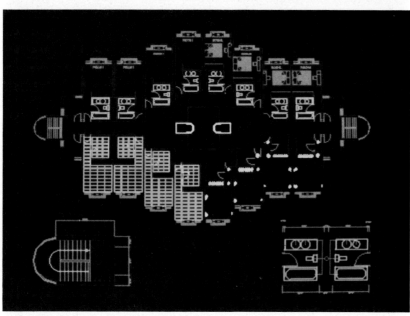

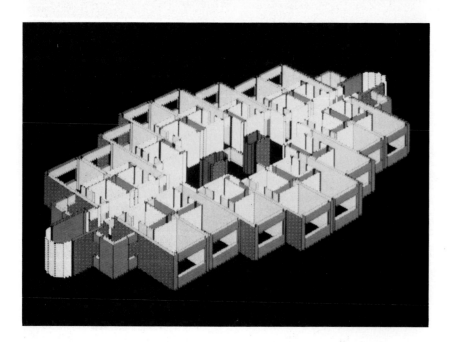

3-D Computer Visualization

Using today's computer capabilities, three-dimensional images of any project can be viewed at any stage of the design development stage. These are generated from the two-dimensional orthographic plans. Using the two-dimensional mode, room outlines and detailed modules are used to investigate alternative schematic options. The final schematic design becomes a detailed drawing by substituting outline modules with detailed modules.

A three-dimensional visualization can be generated from these two-dimensional plans. The viewing height and angle can be adjusted to show any perspective, Three-dimensional modeling is now possible by generating wire frame images and enhancing them with the hidden line removal mode, and surface shading can be added. Instant pan-and-zoom features bring detailed design elements up close for examination. This is a totally new way to communicate your design ideas. For client presentations the dynamic movement of the computer-generated images makes an even more effective simulation of the space than the individual still frames.

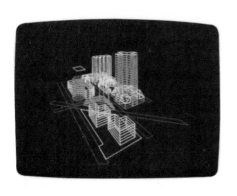 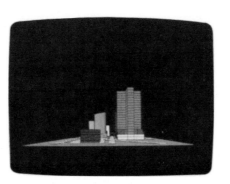 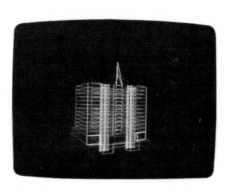

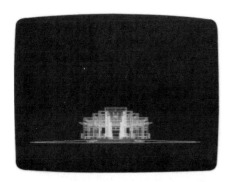 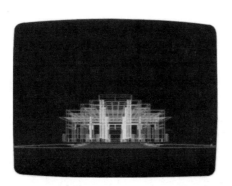 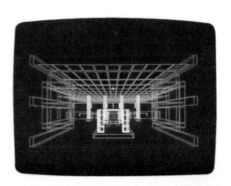

 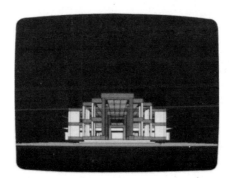 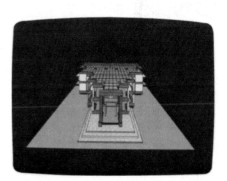

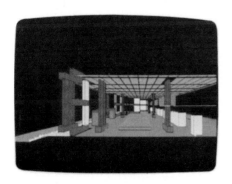 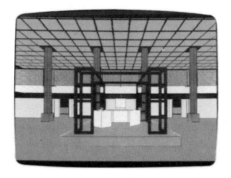 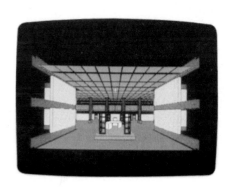

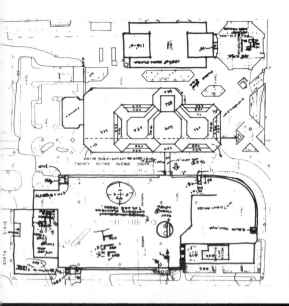

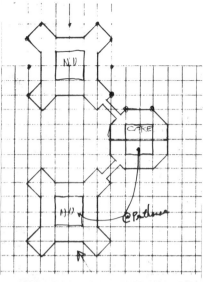

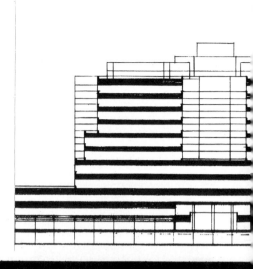

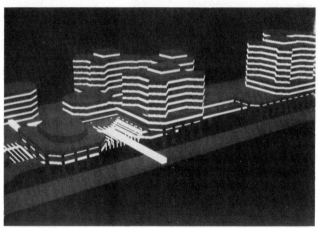

Vanderbilt Hospital

The Vanderbilt Hospital is an addition to an existing structure. The purpose of this study was actually to support preliminary design studies and to visualize different phases of the expansion process.

Although data was received in fragments, the three-dimensional modeling capability of the computer system allowed precise location of the new complexes and the generation of a high-resolution mass model. Once the building data was entered as a three-dimensional database, various views could be generated from any angle in any direction. A sequence of a helicopter flight around the complex was generated, and frames were located according to the "perspective view wheel," allowing specification and location of any view.

PERSPECTIVE

vp13.hop

VIEWS WHEEL

vp2.hop

vp3.hcp

vp4.hcp

vp12.hcp

vp11.hop

vp10.hop

vp5.hop

vp6.hop

vp9.hop

vp8.hop

vp7.hop

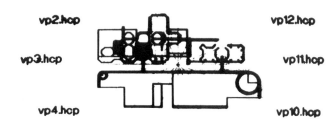

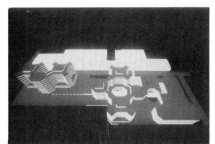

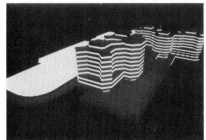

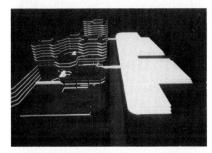

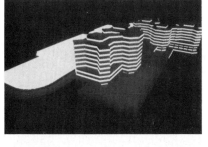

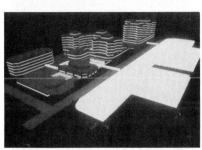

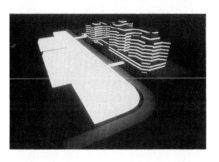

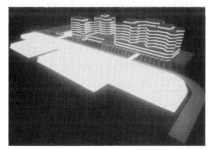

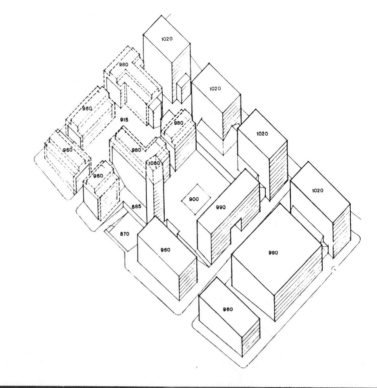

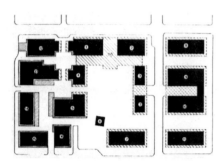

Gateway Plaza

These computer-generated images of an urban project are part of the same one shown in design sketch form on pages 20 and 21. The advantage of the computer-generated images over the design sketches is that urban context can be studied from several aerial angles.

One of the prime study areas was the various roof forms that were to be used throughout the project. By projecting these aerial views on the computer, the designs could be compared. Photos were taken directly off the CAD monitor with a 35mm camera on color negative film. From these negatives, color prints can be made for review and study purposes.

The three-dimensional modeling feature of the computer allows coloration of the different elements of the building. This separation of color makes it more effective for studying shapes, form, and other spatial elements.

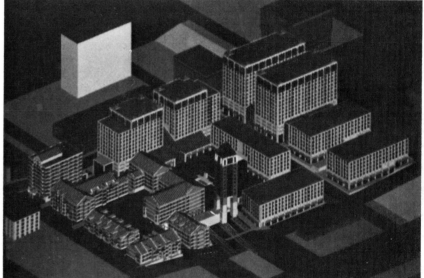

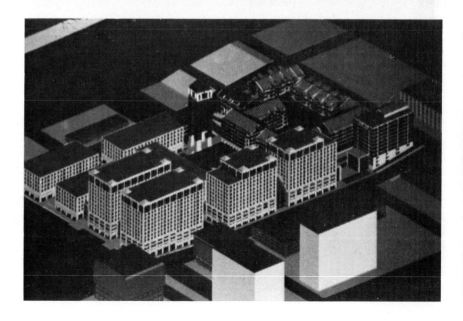

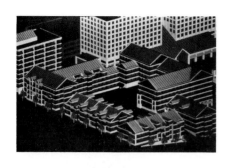
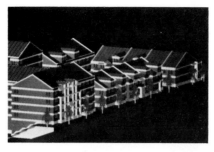

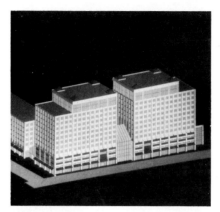

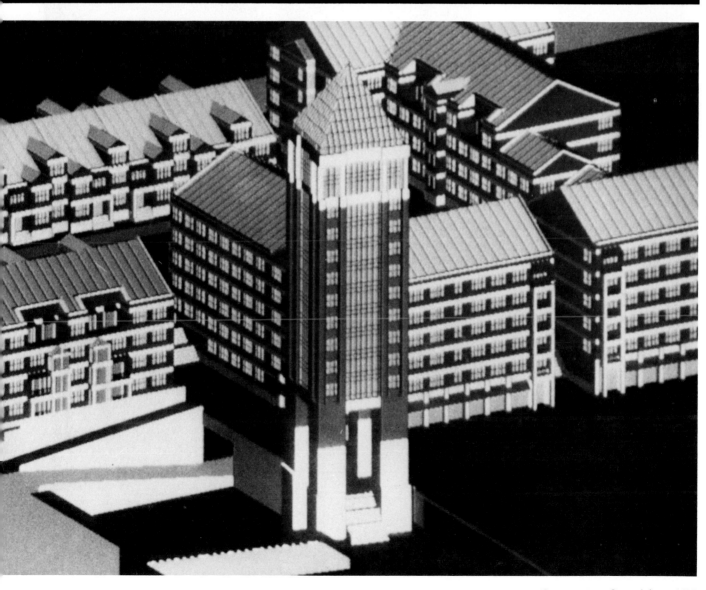

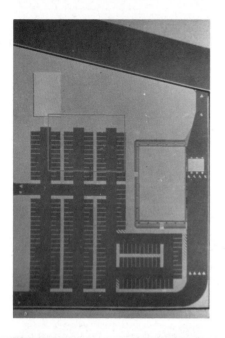

Three-Phase Massing Study

This building massing study was designed for a prototype building system. They specifically used the three-dimensional graphics to enhance their visual presentation of the building. Phase One is the single-story building. Phase Two is shown by the addition of a two-story building adjacent to Phase One. Phase Three is the addition of the second floor to Phase One. The interior of the building was viewed by removing the roof from Phase One. To present the final phase, it was rotated in 40° increments to show the building's symmetry from all perspectives.

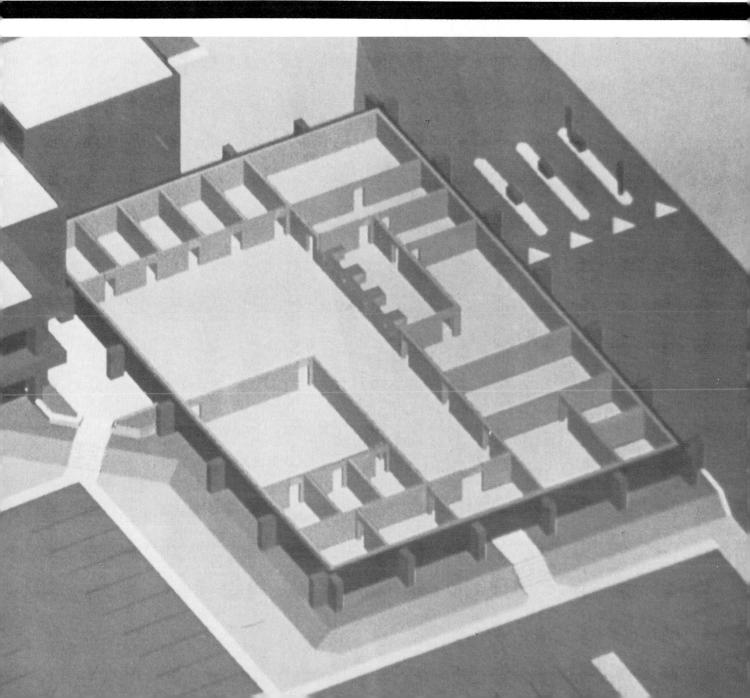

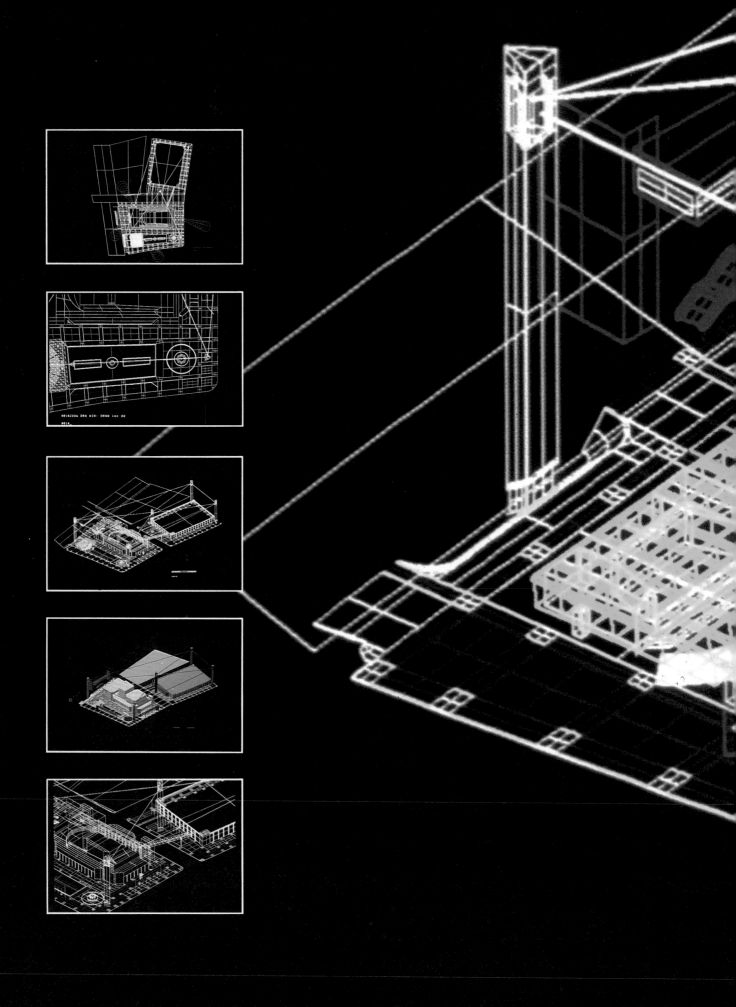

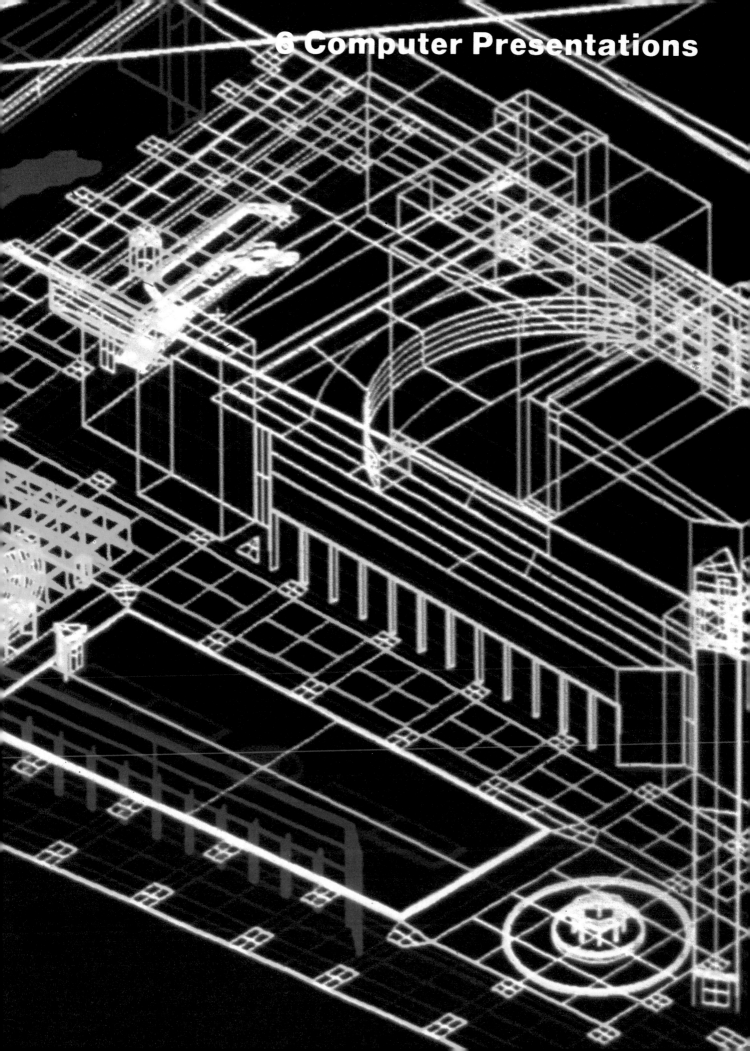

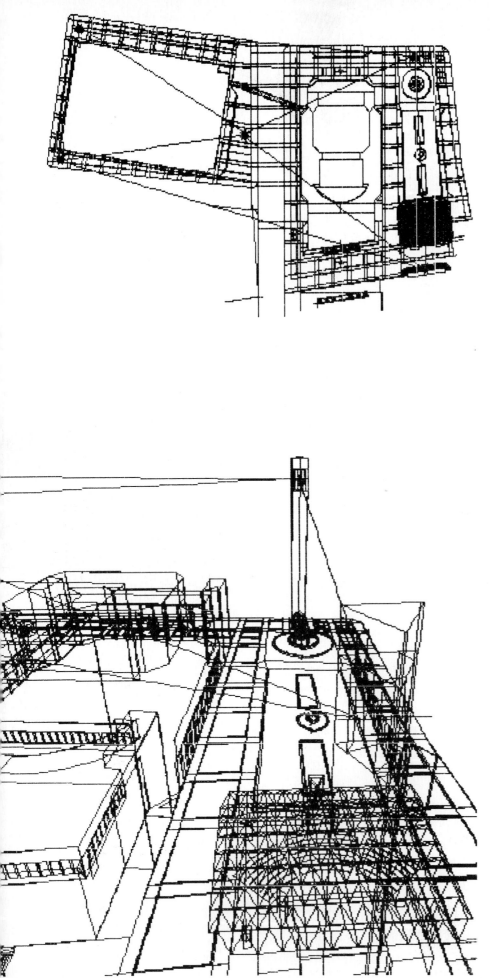

Performing Arts Center

This project was entered in the Environmental Arts Competition whose program was to integrate the variety of structures of the Milwaukee Performing Arts Center. The architects used computers to develop their design.

They used the computer graphics lab of a local technical college to enter the existing design conditions into the computer. These comprised the original building and site arrangements as the architects envisioned them, including the main structure of the center, a horse chestnut grove, a water fountain, the parking structure and overpass, and an outdoor pavilion.

First, the coordinates of the existing site and buildings were entered into the computer and a three-dimensional line model was created. Next, proposed design elements were added, viewed from various vantage points, and evaluated; the heights of the laser towers were adjusted and refined, for example, still in line drawing form.

The scheme they developed was inspired in part by Edmund Bacon's Design of Cities, in which he examines the use of minarets around a mosque as a device for defining space in Islamic architecture—establishing "a transparent cube of space infused with the spirit of the mosque." For the Arts Center, the architects proposed "minarets" (based in form on the column detail of the original building) that would transmit laser beams into the sky, enclosing the site in a staccato-colored ring and creating a holographic effect that would broadcast events at the Center to the entire city. Lighting effects were redoubled in reflective glass entrance arches and in reflecting pools encircling the site, defining the property, tying the site to the Milwaukee River, and reinforcing the formal Islamic theme.

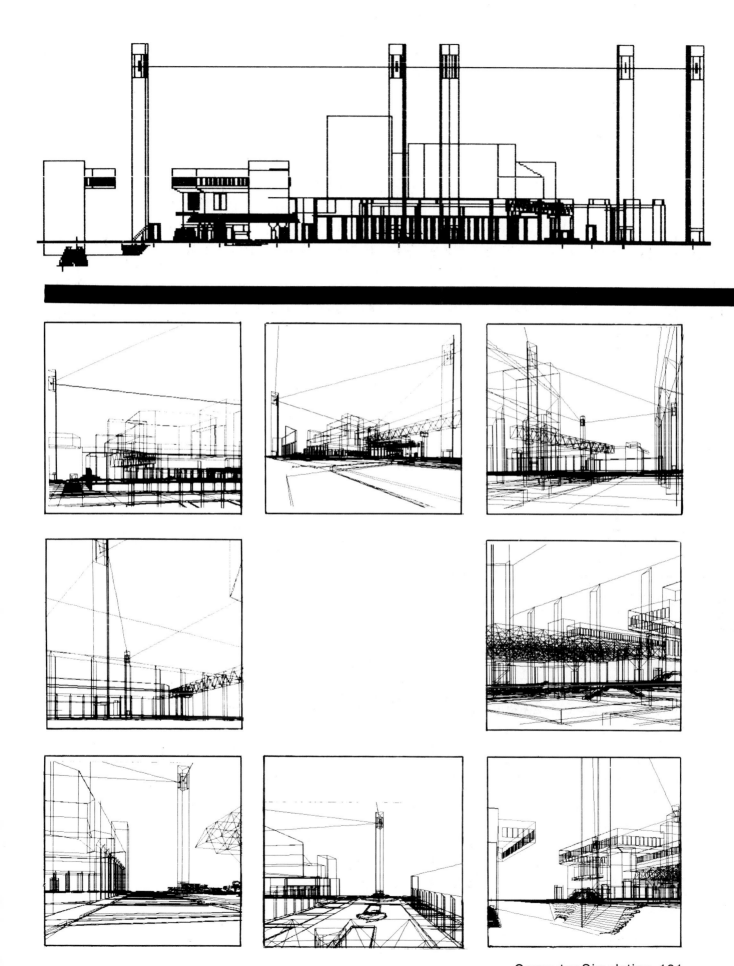

Performing Arts Center

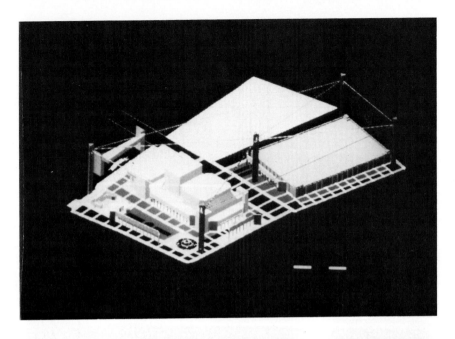

Having developed their design in a three-dimensional line drawing form, they used the data in two ways: to create computer models with solid surfaces, shaded at various sun angles; and to derive dimensioned drawings. Material specifications were added in note form, and parts were refined and reinserted in the overall design.

Reproduction drawings of the PAC grounds were obtained from the City of Milwaukee to provide the accuracy and back-up material needed. A three-dimensional model was established of all existing architectural features. From these models, the architects were able to fully visualize the existing massing and site features. Various schemes were developed in sketch form which were inserted into the database. Evaluating the massing, scale, size, and texture helped to solidify the development of the design. The computer allowed them to clearly evaluate the heights of the laser towers by adjusting them many times until they were finally approved by the design team.

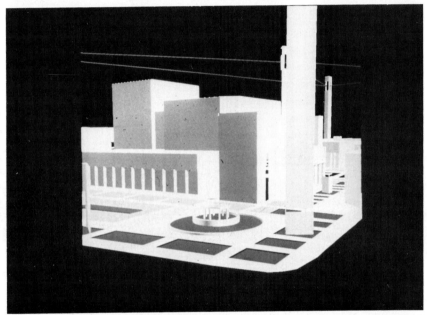

Time was also a major factor in using the computer. For example, the space-frame roof truss on the Peck Pavilion was created in less than six minutes. The architects were then able to look at the space frame from various angles in perspective, from an aerial to a ground view, without reconstructing the initial input.

These concepts were manipulated and enhanced with various colors until they felt comfortable with the design. A variety of perspective images was stored in memory.

Multiple perspectives were reproduced on paper via the plotter. Surfaces were shaded at various sun angles using the solid modeling mode. This was then captured on film from the monitors and mounted on the competition's required boards.

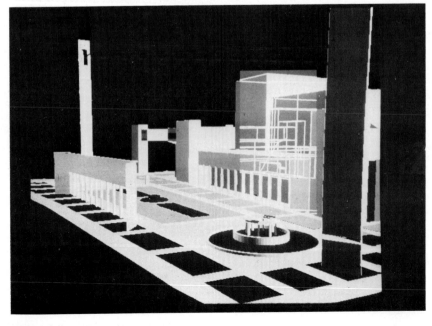

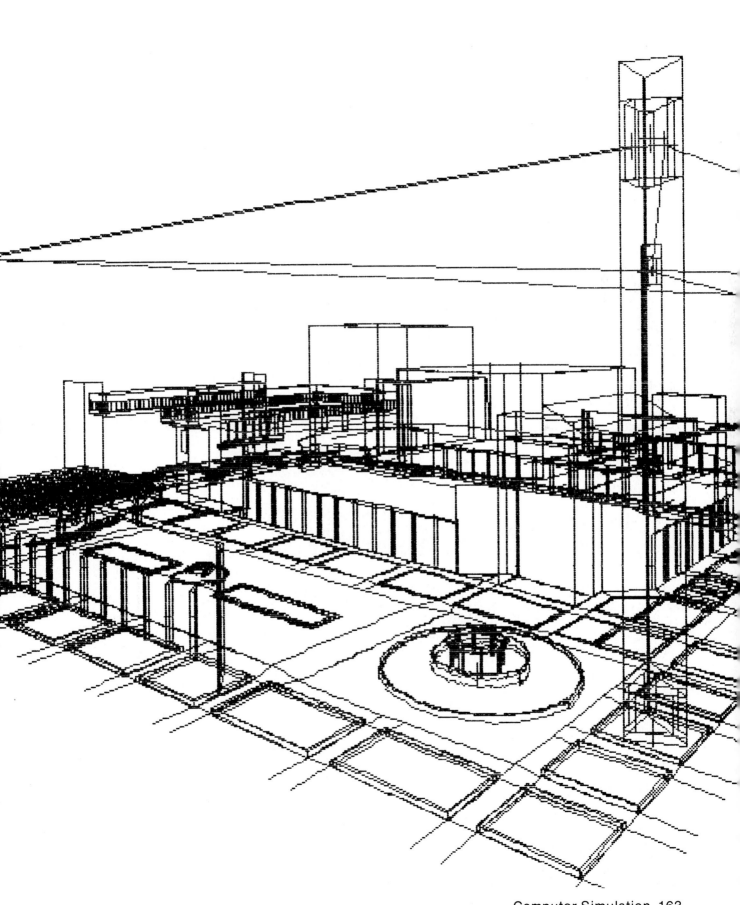

Mt. Washington Campus

A wooded, hilltop campus which served as a Catholic women's college for more than 100 years is being transformed into an ultramodern data processing and educational center for one of the country's largest insurance companies. In addition, a new data processing center and a new education center will be designed.

This computer-drawn design shows how the education and computer centers will tie in with the older buildings on the campus. The computer is used, among other things, to show clients how a variety of design alternatives will look.

A comparison can be made between the photographs of the model and the computer plots. In the views of the interior dining hall the computer even plotted the location of tables and chairs.

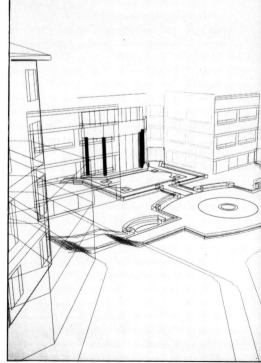

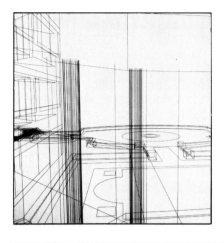

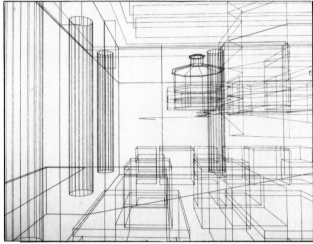

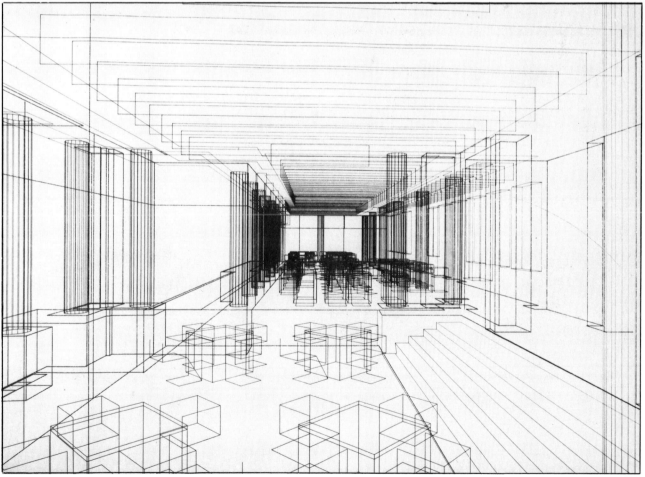

Hospital Project

These perspective drawings show various three-dimensional views of a hospital project. A major concern for this hospital was visibility from the main access roadway to the south, and clear separation of various types of vehicular traffic. An extensive simulation of possible solutions to these problems was done using an integrated computer-aided-design system. The computerized simulation aided in determining the optimum siting for the hospital facility and assisted in the development of clear circulation paths.

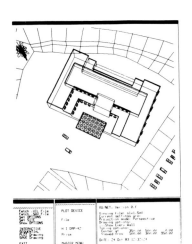

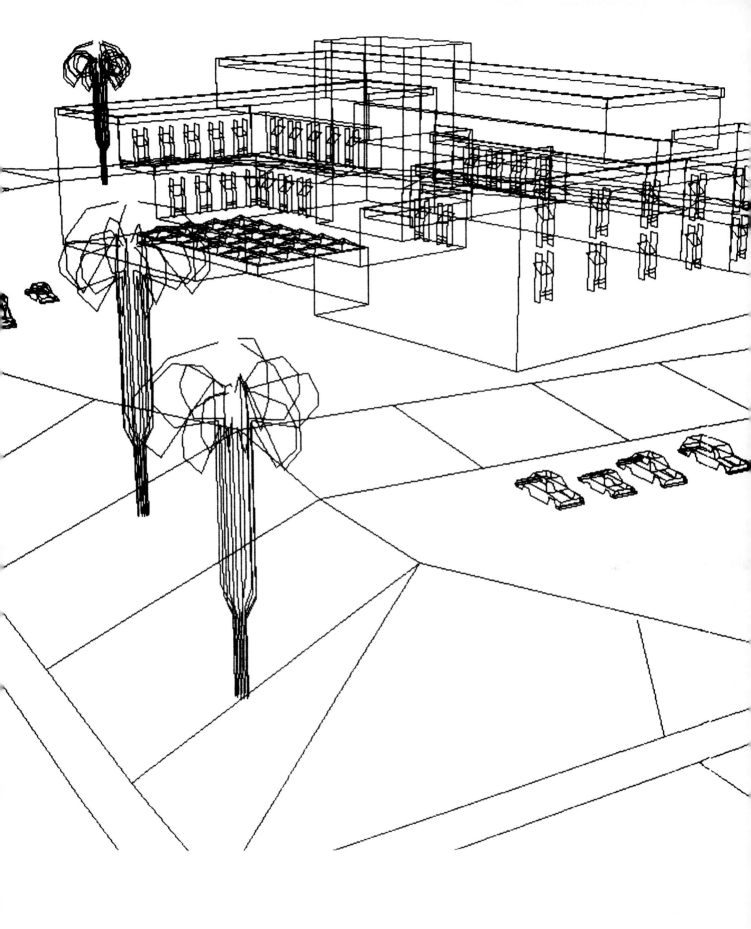

Hospital Project

These two-dimensional drawings demonstrate the layering capabilities of the system. The layering approach allows the architects to minimize the redrawing of a floor plan whenever different information is required. Certain layers, such as walls, dimensions and partitions, can be recalled with other layers that vary, such as plumbing and gases in the top plan, heating in the second, power in the third, and furniture and notations in the bottom plan. The perspective views show the same plan in three dimensions, allowing the designers to rapidly determine the feel of various room configurations as they simulate moving around or even walking through the spaces.

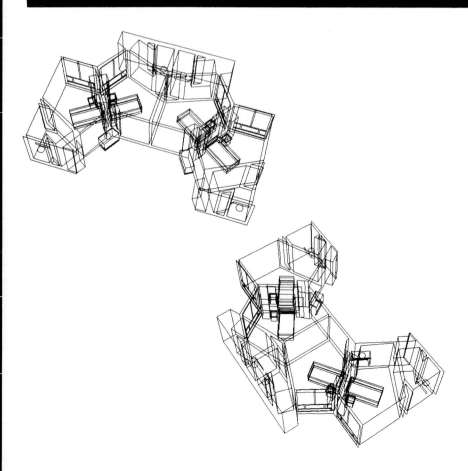

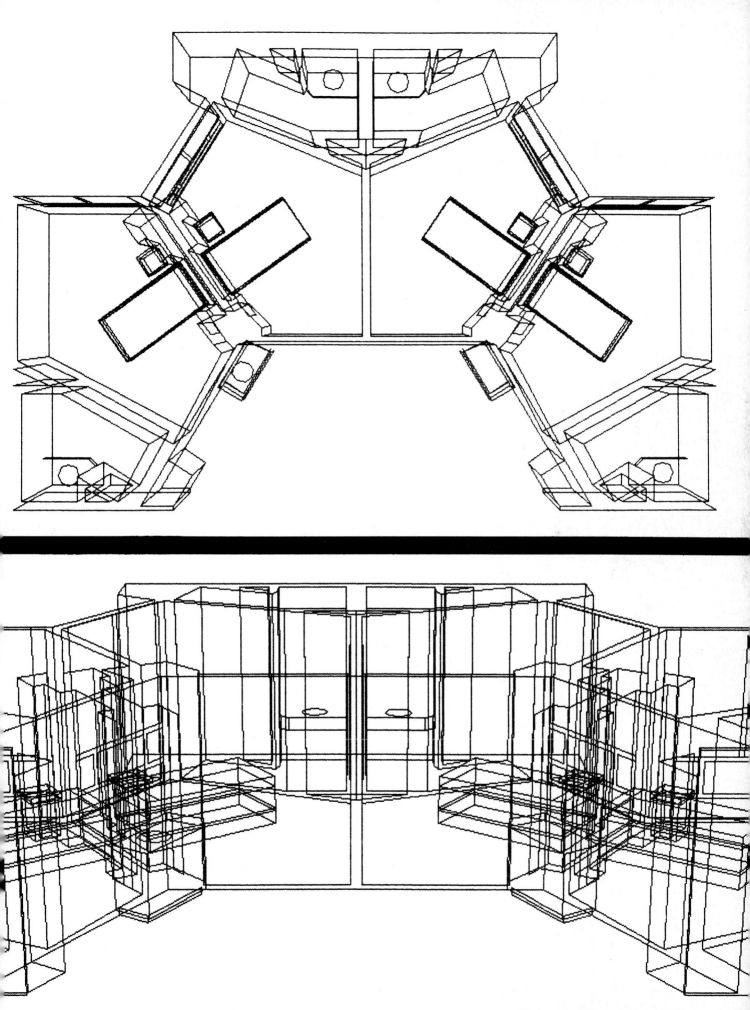

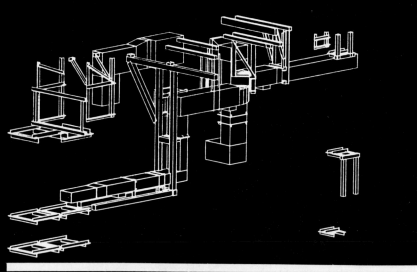

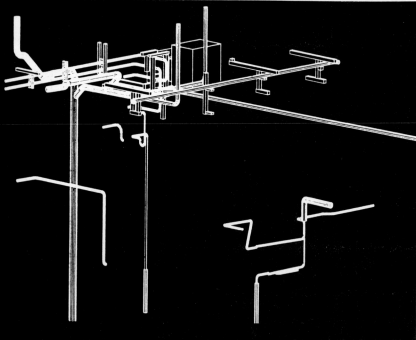

Space Modeling

Computerized plant modeling is becoming a realistic and effective alternative to other modeling methods. The technology exists now, in both hardware and software, to build models of complex plant structures. High-resolution color graphic terminals can display lifelike images of selected model segments in any desired view or content.

Modeling detail and accuracy is completely under the user's control. Individual plant components, such as valves, equipment, instruments, and so forth, can be modeled in a very realistic format. The user can build a library of these components and install them anywhere within the model being constructed. The model can be developed gradually as the design is progressing.

The computerized model is gradually growing and being refined as the design and construction of the project is progressing. Since the computerized model is easily changed and modified, it can provide a focal point of all design and construction of the project.

Two of the most important items of output from the computerized modeling are the production of graphic displays on high-resolution color CRTs and hard-copy drawings produced in color.

Employing the system interactively, the user can display any image generated from the model and point to any component in the view to find more information about that particular component.

If the model includes a graphic display capability and a plant component database, this system becomes a powerful tool for maintenance planning and power plant outage management. The model can accurately represent the "as-built" condition of the plant. Using the graphic system, views of the plant can be generated and stored as part of the project database. These views can be combined with additional information relative to individual components.

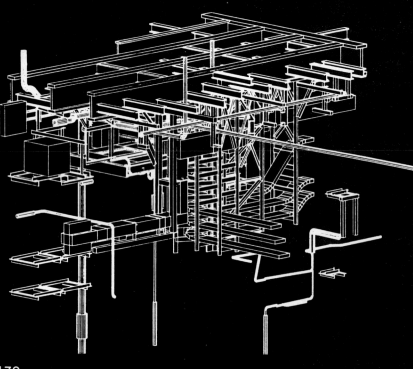

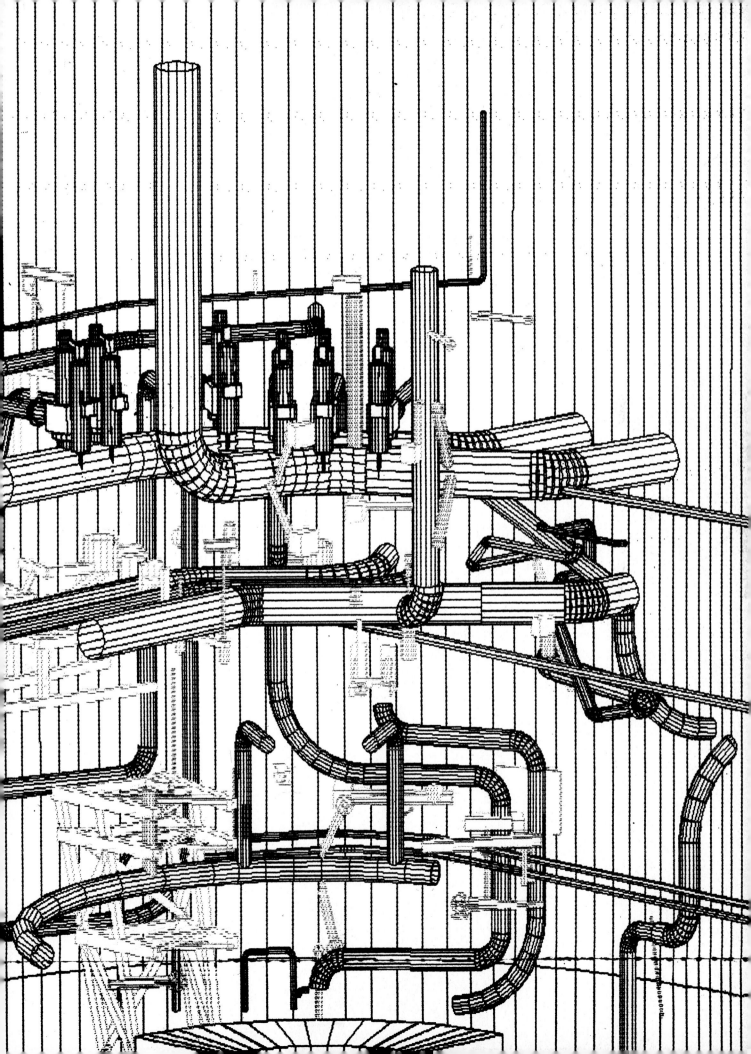

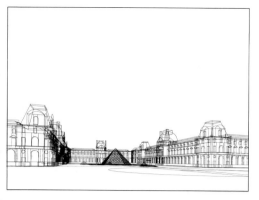 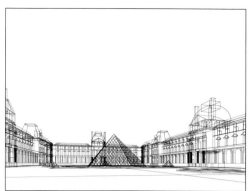 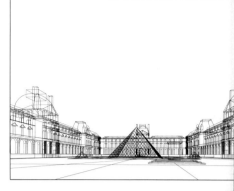

Louvre

One of the most famous museums in the world needed new ancillary space for a main entrance, parking, restaurants, shops and storage. The architects turned to the computer for a method of displaying a unique solution. By entering data from dimensional elevations and site plans into the computer they were able to study a number of design forms before choosing the classic dimensions of the Great Pyramid of Giza. They produced a number of three-dimensional perspective views of the final design, including views from inside the pyramid looking out.

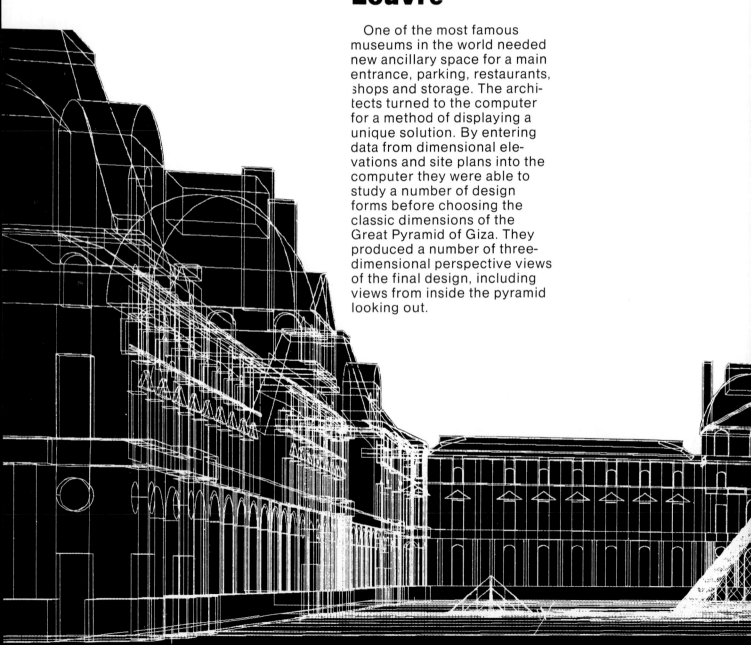

B.C. Place

Take the city of Vancouver and put it in a computer. Digitize all 4,000 buildings, plus streets, parks, waterways, and mountains. Then, use this information to conceptualize a massive 25-year urban development project.

It's the first time anyone ever attempted such a huge task. but, equipped with computer-aided design tools, the task is possible.

With a CADD system it is possible to plot an entire cityscape in three dimensions from any perspective angle. With the database they were able to develop a model of downtown buildings. They could also generate one-, two-, or three-point perspectives of buildings within the city from any desired viewpoint.

Once the initial building outlines were plotted they were cleaned up by a process that removes hidden lines. At the end of this process a solid-looking model of each structure emerges. In addition, other architectural firms have utilized the same services to generate perspectives of proposed buildings within the existing Vancouver landscape at significantly reduced costs.

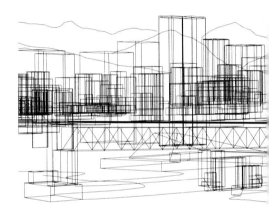

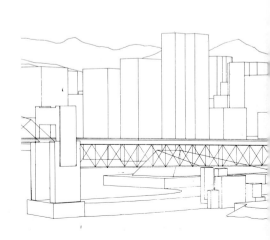

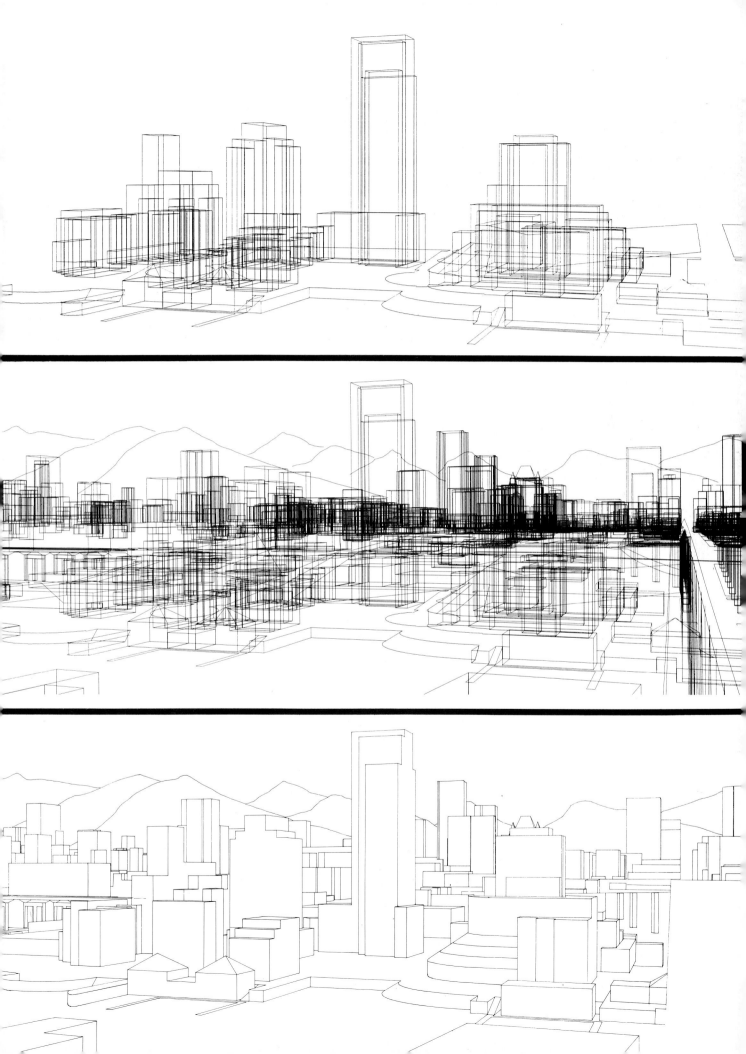

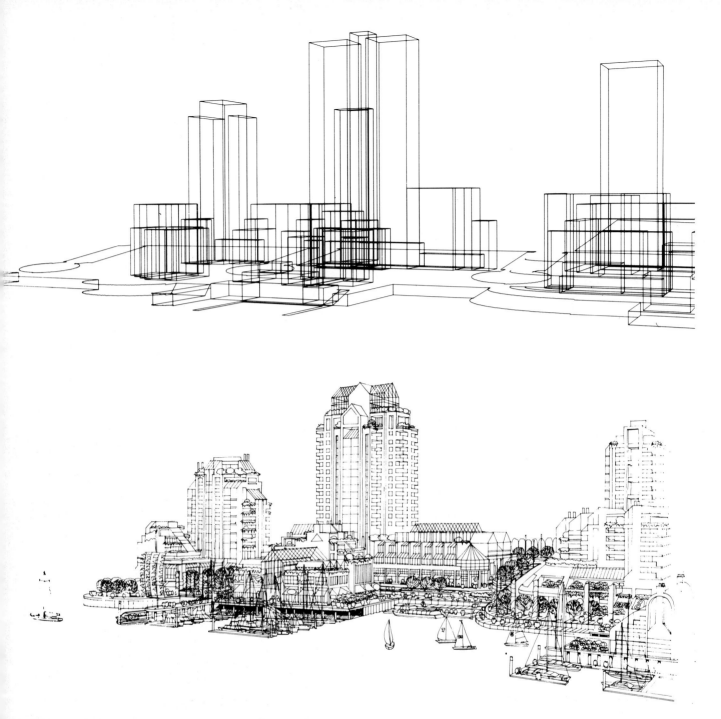

B.C. Place

The basis for this drawing was one of the many computer-generated views for the Expo 86 and B.C. Place project. They are used for design evaluation and presentation to planners. A line drawing of the proposed design was drawn over this computer layout and elements of entourage were added. The drawing was then colored and reduced to the size of a colored site photograph taken from the same perspective angle. The combined drawing was used as a visual aid in discussions with planners and the general public, as to the project's visual impact on the city skyline.

7 Sequential Simulation

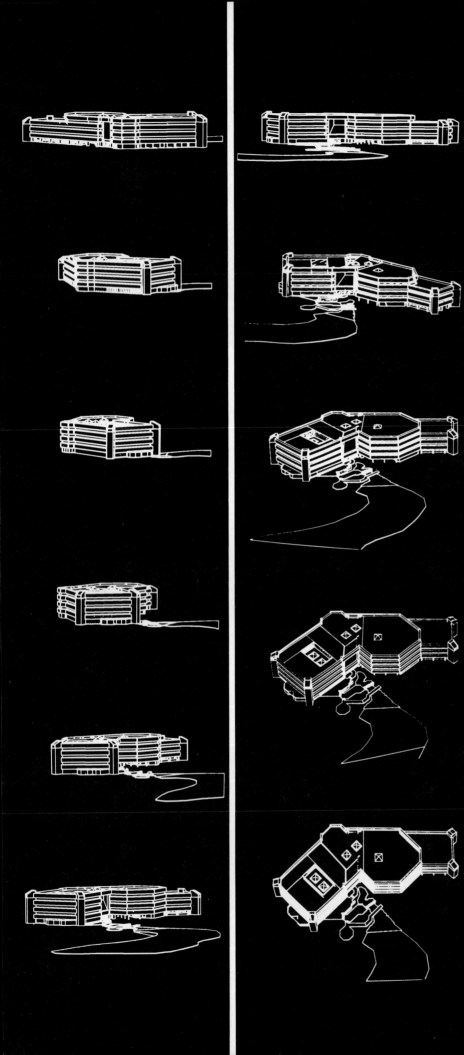

Farm Credit Bank

To help visualize the dramatic setting of the Farm Credit Bank's building and the interior design as it would be seen by a visitor, a videotape sequence of computer-generated drawings simulating the approach to and a walk around the building was developed.

First, they put the design of the bank building in their computer in a three-dimensional mode. Someone suggested taking slides of the three-dimensional images and using them in the presentation in place of a model. After they took a closer look at the slides, they decided to videotape the slide sequence to see if they could add motion to it.

The videotape was created by photographing a number of views of the Farm Credit Bank's building directly off the **CADD** system workstation screen, utilizing a 35mm camera. An in-house procedure was set up to transfer the slides to videotape. Using the technique called "off the wall," they simply copied the projected slides with a home video camera in a half inch (VHS) format. Each slide was taped for about 6-7 seconds. In taping the 60 or more slides, they came up with a minute of videotape.

The videotape was utilized for presentation to the client in lieu of a model or an artist's rendering, or both. It was felt that the dynamics of the videotape would have a favorable impression on the client.

To establish the three-dimensional perspective of the Farm Credit Bank's new building, the two-dimensional conceptual design sketches were placed in a three-dimensional file in basic outline form. This file was then utilized to conduct massing studies, using the solid modeling capability of the computer.

The dynamics of this type of presentation will very likely make the use of models and sketches obsolete.

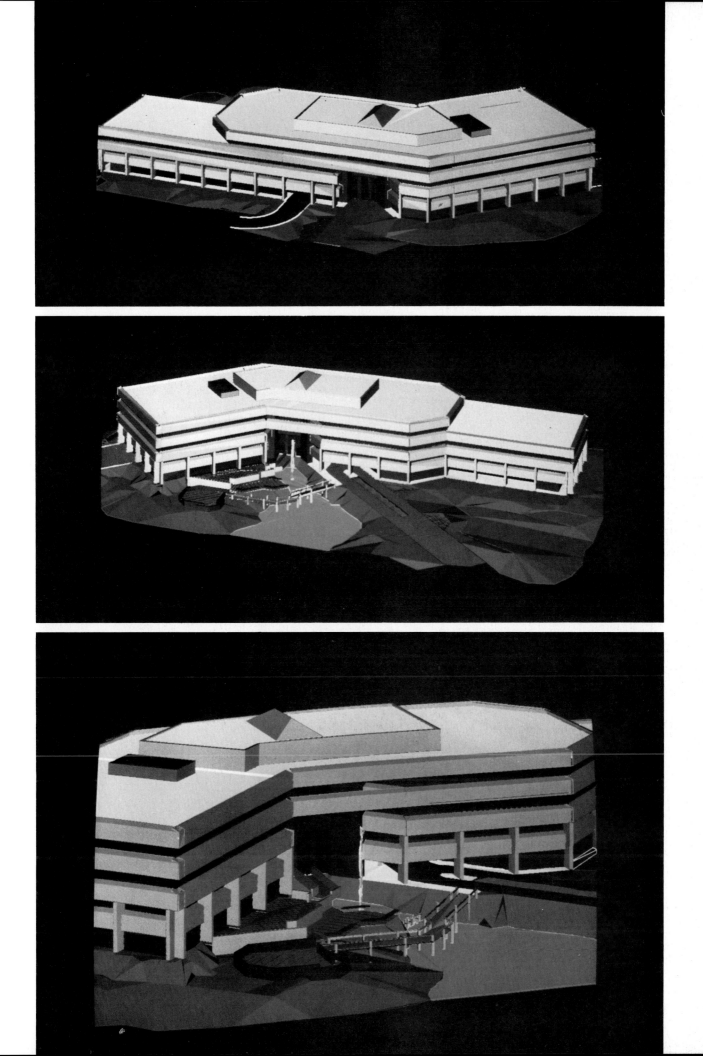

Wolf Trap

When fire destroyed the outdoor theater at Wolf Trap Farm Park in April 1982, plans for its rebuilding began immediately. The design of the new Filene Center was started within weeks of the destruction and working drawings were completed four months later—an achievement made possible by the architect's computer-aided design and drafting capabilities.

The design was drawn on a new advanced CADD workstation. The film was taken from the system's CRT as the design was rotated, panned, and zoomed in and out to depict the proposed design from many different perspectives.

The firm intended to update plans of the old theater, which had burned down, using conventional drafting methods. By the original estimate, the job would take 12 months. The client, however, set a four-month deadline for the design phase. The company was left with two choices: hire about a half dozen more drafters or put their CADD system, out of the box for only three weeks, into action.

The CADD system was used because it gave the architects the drafting power to turn out high-quality drawings in the minimum amount of time. To complete the project on schedule, drafters worked three shifts, 24 hours a day on two workstations, turning out 66 drawings covering basic design, structural components, and floor plans. Only plans for plumbing, electrical work, and mechanical equipment were drafted by hand.

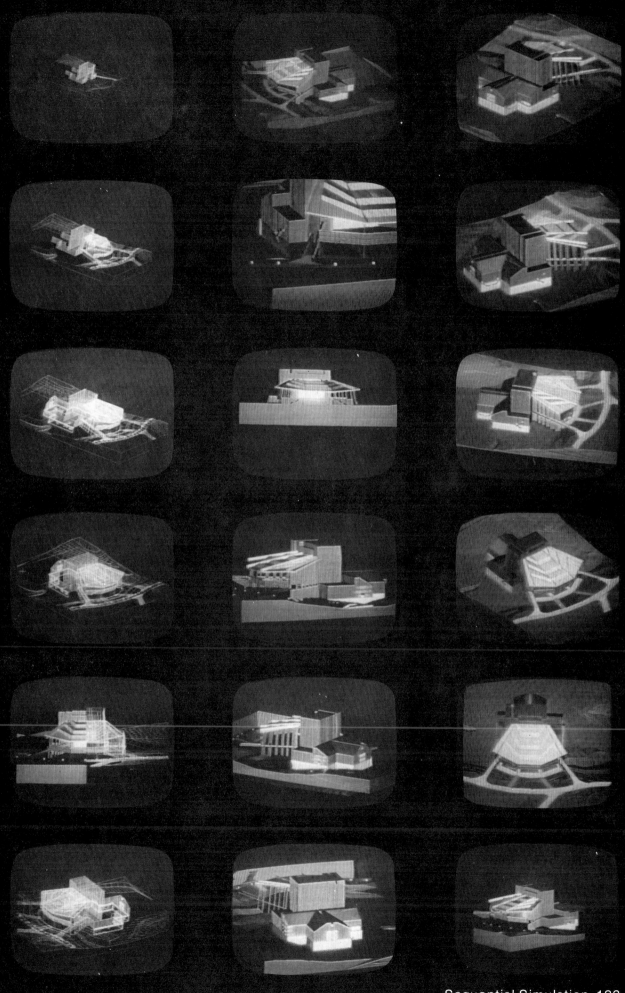

Nabisco

This video was prepared to demonstrate a design scheme and approach to the new Nabisco Technology Center.

The architects combined several techniques within the video format. They showed models, renderings, the site, and live action scenes from design meetings in their office. The major part of the video was produced using computer-generated images photographed off the CADD monitor. Animated drawings described the function of the building.

Quality has always been central to the growth of Nabisco and Standard Brands. We know too that since their recent merger this emphasis has been re-doubled. We are here to support Nabisco Brands in its commitment to technology by creating a highly advanced new product research and development facility at a site where the company now maintains offices.

Our solution is intended to help Nabisco Corporate Technology Group meet its threefold mission. One—to ensure the highest quality of Nabisco Brand products. Two—to provide the core technology required to maintain company leadership in production and marketing. Three—to create new products through technological innovation for future growth of the company.

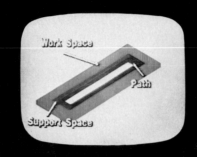

In meeting these three objectives, cost effectiveness is of course crucial in terms of first costs and life-cycle costs. First, let's consider productivity. We begin with a universal work space that's uninterrupted and open-ended.

The next step is to organize these three zones into an efficient and cost effective form. A donutlike arrangement offers many advantages. Its compactness helps minimize distances. The core provides space for community interaction and, by keeping all work areas on the perimeter, we can take advantage of natural light and exterior views.

Now we address mechanical servicing of the building. Again the key is flexibility because a highly adaptable service system is the single most important factor in the building's capacity for change and growth.

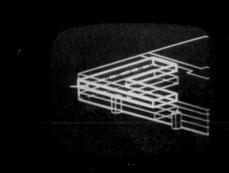
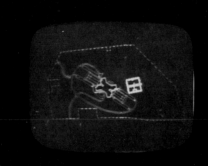

This system minimized cost in two ways. Those areas that do not need services initially need not be outfitted until necessary. Down the line, operating costs will be significantly reduced because the separate service zones allow the system to be freely changed and maintained without disrupting working floors.

Our second design objective, site responsiveness, also plays a role in developing the final design. Our planning begins with a search for the ideal building location.

We start by analyzing the opportunities and constraints posed by site conditions, eliminating areas that have steep slopes, poor soil, or vegetation worthy of preservation. Next we identify areas that pose zoning complications and consider adjacent land uses and possible future site development. The building is then placed on the optimum location to take advantage of pleasing views.

The successful design of such a facility depends on integrating tangible goals, such as creating productive work spaces and incorporating advanced systems and equipment, with intangible objectives, such as improving work flow, heightening the exchange of scientific ideas, and attracting employees and encouraging them to stay.

According to the firm's partner in charge of research facility design, "Unless a facility is highly flexible and expandable, it will not in the long term remain productive." We can achieve unprecedented capabilities for growth and change using a concept we call "universal space"—the ability of any area within the building to ultimately serve any purpose.

We'll examine the technology center's design in terms of three critical goals: One—creating an efficient and productive work environment; Two—designing a facility which is site responsive; and Three—developing an appropriate building image.

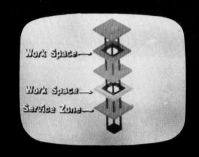 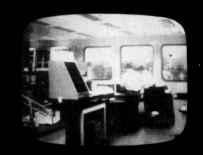 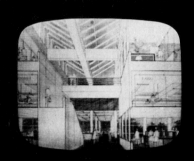

The technology center's program embodies both offices and laboratory functions. We can therefore realize the benefit of reduced site coverage by stacking these two functions on separate floors.

These then feed into horizontal distribution networks separate from the working floors. These service zones are located beneath the first floor, above the second floor, and most important, in a full-height interstitial service zone. Finally, we examine how this facility can meet its third important performance criterion—conveying an appropriate message to employees, the community, and the corporate world.

We therefore developed a central street to serve as a commons or meeting ground. In addition to encouraging communication, this street provides a focal point for the facility, adds architectural interest, and creates a sense of community.

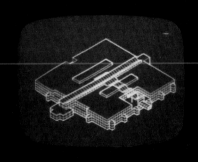  

Offices can be converted into labs. Extensions may be added to the building. New generation mechanical systems can be installed, all with a minimum of disruption and expense.

Another need for a healthy scientific environment is a quiet place to think. Such places are provided in glass-enclosed rooms on the building's perimeter. Our ideal flexible structure can now be configured and outfitted to meet the specific needs of your program in terms of adjacencies, equipment, and work floor. As these needs change and grow, the facility can easily change and grow with them.

In order to project Nabisco's own sense of quality and achievement, this building must convey a high degree of architectural excellence. An essential beauty and sense of perfection emerge from this facility's rational response to both the tangible and intangible realities of research and development operation.

First Center

Once a project is designed, it must be leased to tenants. This is the subject of this video, which utilizes sequential trips through an architectural model mixed with realistic natural scenes to make it appear as if the building is already constructed.

This technique is used to sell tenants but it can also be used to present the design to the client because the emphasis is placed on the end user of the facility.

They call it World Headquarters Row for a very good reason. Because the companies you'll find here read like a who's who of corporate giants: Gulf & Western, IBM, Travelers, Prudential, AMC, Bendix, All State, Macabee. Now soon you'll be able to join this prestigious lineup of corporations here on Headquarters Row because First Center is coming.

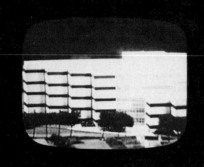
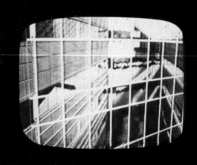

Your eye is immediately captured by three connecting atriums. The six buildings, each separated by an atrium, provide flexibility for six signature buildings. A combination of varying roof lines, ranging from two to six stories, contributes to the individual building identity while still maintaining the overall design harmony.

In addition, the design provides for up to ten exterior corner offices on each floor.

Now, share an exciting visual experience as we enter Phase I. Once inside, you'll be amazed. Because we managed to bring the outside inside. You're over-

You're surrounded by towering trees and lush greenery. You're invited to do some shopping, some browsing. How

about lunch? Or you can do your banking. Don't worry about the weather. We're inside, remember?

Ahead, a large reflecting pool invites casual conversation, a place to meet. A glass-enclosed elevator will provide a commanding view high above the atrium of Phases 2 and 3.

186

First Center, an existing new three-phase office development that explodes with light and space and that just might be the largest office development to be built in this decade. First Center, an office development so unique it's already hailed as a mid-rise landmark.

First Center, a dramatic design concept that offers the image, prestige, and amenities of a world class office building.

As you approach, First Center provides a striking visual image, spiraling out of 30 acres of parklike landscape.

whelmed by a feeling of spaciousness, room, freedom. Look up— aerial bridges make travel between buildings easy, convenient, and unique.

First Center will provide the atmosphere conducive to the quality of worklife so essential to today's modern office. Now, take a stroll along an enclosed pedestrian avenue. It's like outdoor living without ever stepping outside.

No need to go outdoors—just cross a bridge. The feeling of spaciousness and freedom continues with First Center office space. One can enjoy the outdoor scenery. There are plenty of windows to capture your attention.

Inside and outside, First Center provides a vibrant stimulating environment, but it also does more. With a Phase 1 capacity of 250,000 square feet and an additional 500,000 square feet with all phases, First Center allows you to plan

for the future by providing expansion capability under the convenience of one roof. Think about it. As part of Phase 1 you can expand and grow as First Center expands and grows.

First Center is more than just office space. First Center is an address of distinction, where you can enjoy the stature, prestige, and image of a world class office building.

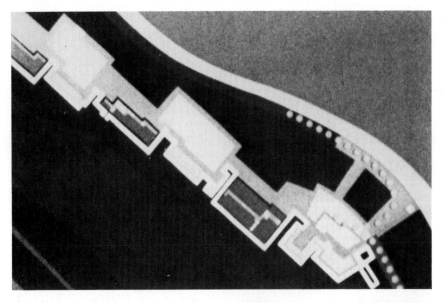

F.D.R. Memorial

Many attempts were made to select a design for a permanent memorial to Franklin Delano Roosevelt in the nation's capital, even though a site had been set aside for more than twenty years. When a design scheme was finally selected, the team began to make plans for presenting the process to the Parks Commission using the techniques of a 16mm film simulation of a walk through the memorial.

The design began with the search for what a memorial should be in our time rather than copying Greek or Roman temples. And the memorial had to overcome the relatively "unstructured" site. The scheme evolved to conceptually include four garden rooms, which were symbolic of the four stages of life and four freedoms that FDR professed.

Throughout the sequences, water is used dominantly because of the importance FDR placed on it. Waterfalls were not as appropriate as rivulets, jets and planes of water, and the major culminating event was the amphitheater which is open to the tidal basin.

To portray the spaces within the memorial, an elaborate trip was planned using a 16mm movie camera. The film opened with scenes of the selected artisans and designers moving blocks of materials around, building statues, and sculpting bronze reliefs. The activity was so realistically portrayed by the film that the impression was given that they were constructing the project, when, in fact, they were constructing a very realistic model.

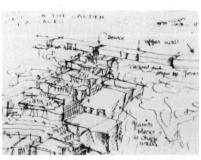

Once the camera was inside the model, the viewer was on a journey through each of the four garden rooms, experiencing views of the fountains and waterfalls. The effect of the simulated trip was so realistic that viewers were not certain whether they had just seen a movie of a miniature environment, or the real thing.

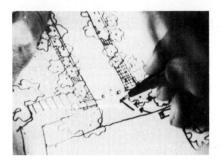

Aspen Project: Videodisc Simulation

For centuries, newcomers to unfamiliar environments have had to rely on maps, diagrams, and verbal descriptions to find their way around.

There is a new form of spatial representation that can be created which substitutes for the actual experience. This medium, called the interactive movie map, provides a mechanism for pre-experiencing an unfamiliar locale.

The interactive movie map is a computer-controlled, video-disc-based system which displays two representations of an environment—as "travel land" and as "map land." The user explores both worlds interactively.

In the travel land mode the user "drives" around familiarizing himself or herself with the space by seeing real footage previously filmed on location. This is called surrogate travel. The operator has complete control over speed, direction of travel, direction of view, route selection, and may even choose a season of year in which to view the space. In addition, the user can access pictures of individual building facades and see slide shows and facsimile data about each location.

In the map land mode, the user "helicopters" above aerial overviews of variable scale (and resolution) with customized navigational aids. Such aids include position pointers and route plotters.

With this dynamic overview, the user is able to manipulate the viewpoint above the surface (using track and zoom) and change the modality of representation by flipping between map and photo.

A site was chosen to meet certain criteria suggested by experience: it had to be manageable in size, geographically bounded, and visually differentiated with distinctive landmarks. Aspen, Colorado, was chosen for satisfying

these conditions. The town site, with an area of about one square mile, has only three routes of access. It is bounded on three sides by rivers and on the fourth by a mountain. Mountain ranges visible in several directions provide unique exterior marks. Equally important are a number of additional properties: the street plan is a regular, rectangular grid oriented to the four cardinal directions. A unique geographical feature is that the major mountain landmarks also line up with the cardinal directions of the streets.

Aerial photos were possible by using the local airport. Another advantage of this site was the seasonal variations, which can drastically alter the perception of the space.

Filming of the town was divided into three categories: street travel, aerial overview, and cultural access. The first category included all ground-level movement through the street network of the town; the

second all aerial movement above the town, recorded in aerial photos and overview maps; and the third spatial data on cultural sequences associated with every landmark in town.

Street footage was filmed by driving the center of every street in both directions. Turn footage was taken by making every turn from each street onto every intersecting street.

The cameras were oriented so that the field of view covered up to an entire 360° horizontal panorama. The town was shot in different seasons (fall and winter), different weather conditions (sunny, overcast, and snowing) and at different hours (day and night). The entire town, consisting of 20 miles of streets, was filmed three separate times—fall 1978, winter 1978-79, and fall 1979. Total footage in each case included 15,000 frames for straight sequences and 12,000 frames for turns.

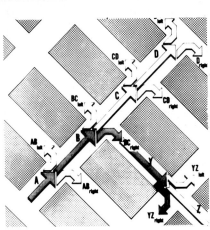

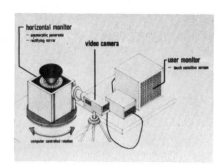

Aspen Project
Videodisc Simulation

The 16mm film was shot at a regular spatial (rather than temporal) interval, one frame every 10 feet. The 10-foot interval was an arbitrarily determined distance that would allow all the footage to fit within the 50,000 frames on one side of a single videodisc. The mechanism used to trigger the cameras at regular spatial intervals was a bicycle wheel trailing the filming rig.

Material from all of the categories described was edited and transferred to an optical videodisc, mostly consisting of 16mm film. Other formats included 35mm movie film and a 2-inch quad videotape. In all, four discs were mastered. The first, with the full 54,000 frames, had the complete surrogate travel footage. It also had facade pictures, slide shows, and extensive cinema footage. The second and third discs were largely experimental. The former included both fall and winter surrogate travel and the various tests of side camera angles. The latter consisted of a catalog of ancillary cultural data plus examples of the first version of QADAS footage. The fourth disc was truly comprehensive, including street travel (different seasons), aerial overviews, facades (different seasons), cultural access (both slide shows and cinema), QADAS animation (version two), 360° anamorphic panoramas, computer-synthesized turns, and the visitor's introduction to the locale.

Aspen Project
Videodisc Simulation

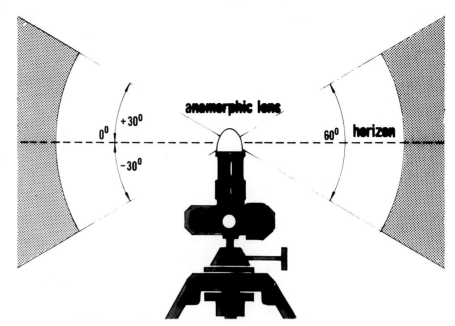

An alternative film format also used for the entire town was the anamorphic "Volpi" lens mounted on a 35mm film camera pointing straight up. This lens recorded a 360° panorama of the scene extending from 30° above the horizon to 30° below onto a ring.

A separate and more comprehensive computer-generated graphics system was developed to show an abstracted representation of the town from any viewpoint—QADAS, or Quick and Dirty Animation System, as it was affectionately nicknamed.

The database was entered from topographical maps by tablet, digitizing the X and Y coordinates of the base corners of each building in Aspen. Height was approximated according to number of stories, determined by visual inspection of previously shot travel footage.

Computer animation views are illustrated on the right. The bottom picture illustrates three modes of representation: the underlying wire frame structure, displayed using hidden lines with smooth shading; solidly colored polygonal shapes; and polygons with photographic texture. Photographic texture was added to selected building facades to enhance the degree of visual realism. (Background mountains were represented by defining them as facades standing far in the distance.) The procedure was to digitize images of the more prominent landmarks and "clean them up" to remove deep shadows and obstructions like bushes or cars. As QADAS drew one of these buildings, it mapped the stored photograph onto the perspective rendering of the facade. This "billboarding" process treated the facade as a two-dimensional surface, ignoring perspective transformation of any features with depth, like porches, awnings, and windowsills.

Comparisons between an original scene and the computer-generated version with perspective billboarding are shown to the right.

The material produced to provide access to examples of local culture included slide shows, short cinema films, and sound recordings. To provide a transition from surrogate travel to this ancillary data, separate pictures were shot of each building in Aspen. With the use of 35mm cameras, 2,000 facades (including parks and other undeveloped sites) were photographed in both fall and winter with matching registration technique, based on verbal descriptions spoken into a portable tape recorder each time a facade picture was shot. In the fall the photographer described exactly how the picture was being centered with reference to fiducial marks on the viewfinder focusing screen, where he or she was standing, and what focal length was being used. In the winter the photographer listened to the tape recording as he or she reshot the same facades, carefully following the directions from the first outing.

Historical registration was created where possible. For scenes where historical photos existed from the turn of the century, modern-day facades were reshot to match the original views.

The interiors of hundreds of sites in Aspen were photographed separately with a 35mm camera to capture a sense of the cultural activity behind the facades of the more interesting locations in town. In addition to 6,000 shots taken on site, printed matter—menus, brochures, and newspaper clippings—was collected and later copied as elaboration on the slide shows. In the case of both slide shows and film, sound was recorded in conjunction with the visuals. Special cases of audio included experiments with verbally guided tours by local residents as well as binaural sound to recreate the characteristic ambience of the space.

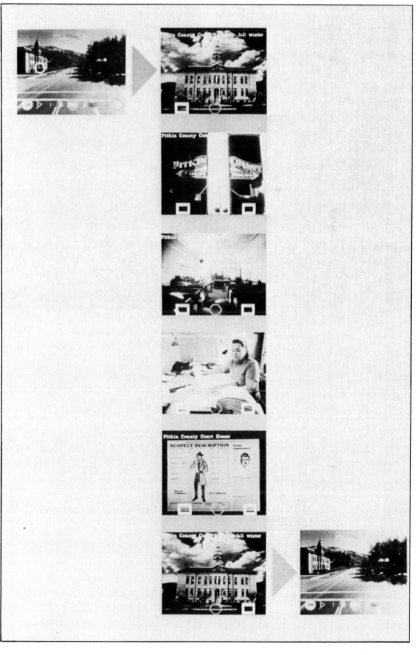

Aspen Project
Videodisc Simulation

The human-machine interface is achieved by providing simple but powerful controls in a multichannel user station that includes pictures, sound, text, and graphics on a touch-sensitive television screen.

The host machine was a 32-bit Perkin-Elmer minicomputer, which was standard hardware in the Architecture Machine Group Lab.

Output from the computer was directed to a number of audio and video devices. The key component was the reflective optical videodisc, with a storage capacity of up to 54,000 frames.

The focal point of the user station was the color video monitor which displayed the movie map images. It had a touch-sensitive screen. This screen, recording the X-Y position of a touching finger, was the user's interface for controlling the journey through the movie map. The station included audio speakers.

In a typical situation, the user sits in front of a touch-sensitive television screen that shows a picture much like what would be seen through the front windshield of a car. Touching the speed control initiates movement down the street. By pushing another button, the user changes course and turns down a side street. Now the user selects a perpendicular view out of the side window. Next, he calls up

a map of the town which traces out the path which he has been following and permits him to decide on a subsequent route. Touching any point on the map causes it to zoom into a detailed area. The user switches the mode of representation between street map, landmark map, and aerial photograph. Whether in map land or travel land, when he wants more information about a landmark of interest, the user touches the building on the screen and is presented with the facade.

The instrument control panel, which the viewer used to engage in surrogate travel, was a computer-generated overlay. Direction of movement was determined by

the blue-green bars flanking the stop sign. In response, the visible videodisc was step-framed at a variable rate up to 10 fps, or an apparent speed of 7 mph. Backing up was achieved by simply stepping the videodisc in reverse.

The arrow at the end served as a "you-are-here" pointer. Selecting the route button from the menu on the left allowed the user to trace out a route he or she wanted to follow when surrogate travel was resumed. This autopilot mode involved a chauffeur to guide the surrogate passenger around. On the schematic map, the prescribed path, traced in red, turned green, block by block, as the trip unfolded. Zooming in for a more detailed view of any part of the map was initiated by touching an intersection in the desired area.

In many cases, a season knob, which was toggled by pushing the appropriate time of year, caused the scene to alternate between fall and winter in perfect registration. The leaves vanished, the snow appeared, but all permanent fixtures remained precisely in place. Finally the user could "stop in for a quick visit" by starting the slide show. The sequence could be stopped or reversed at any point.

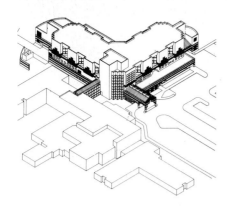

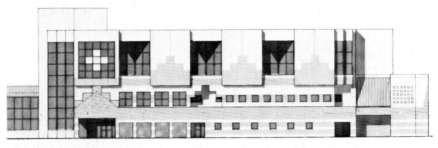

Altus Hospital

There were several methods used to depict this structure in the early stages of preliminary design. There was the traditional set of rendered elevations and an aerial axonometric. In addition there was a low level aerial colored rendering which outlined the building form. Finally, there was a three-dimensional detailed design model that showed the relationship of the new facility to the existing medical structures on the site. Photography of the completed structure from ground level emphasized the unusual features of the building.

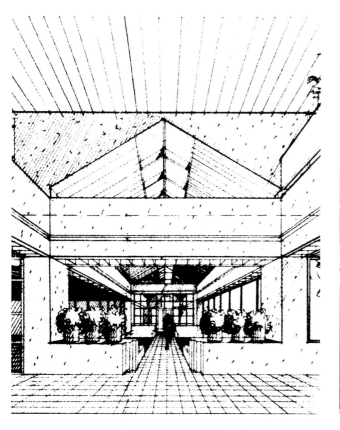

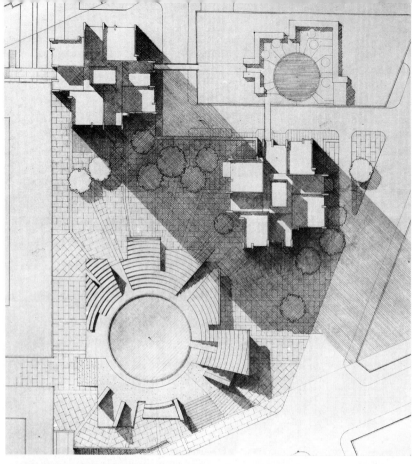

Charles Towers

Original presentation drawings included site plans and floor plans combined with model photography. The model was photographed to coincide with some of the original site drawings. The study models were also shot from elevational viewpoints, which can be compared to the final photographs of the completed building.

The similarity between the original presentation material and the finished project is noticeable.

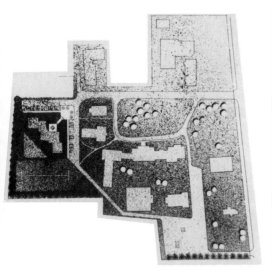

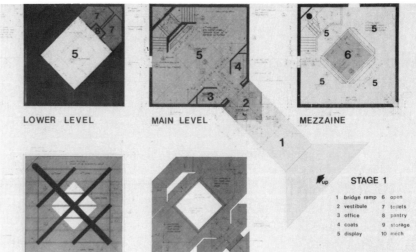

LOWER LEVEL **MAIN LEVEL** **MEZZAINE**

STAGE 1

1 bridge ramp 6 open
2 vestibule 7 toilets
3 office 8 pantry
4 coats 9 storage
5 display 10 mech

Art Gallery

These drawings were prepared for the Westbrook College Fine Arts Gallery and show the various functions of the space.

Future expansion is indicated in plans showing Phase 2 and Phase 3 configuration. The axonometric drawing illustrates, through a detailed cutaway, the initial phase.

The presentation included rough study models, which featured a cutaway section that exposed the interior space. A floor cutout in the second level allows natural light to filter from a central roof skylight. The gallery forms a cube situated on a flat grassy plane. The building's form is well illustrated in the photograph of the completed project.

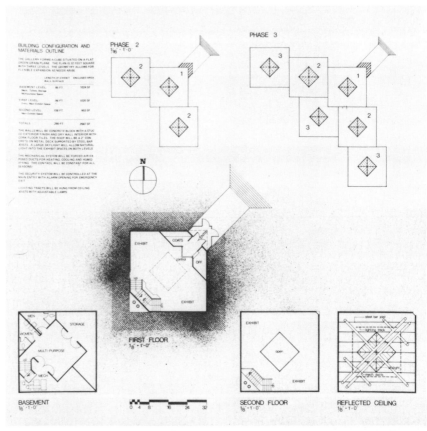

BUILDING CONFIGURATION AND MATERIALS OUTLINE

PHASE 2   PHASE 3

FIRST FLOOR

BASEMENT   SECOND FLOOR   REFLECTED CEILING

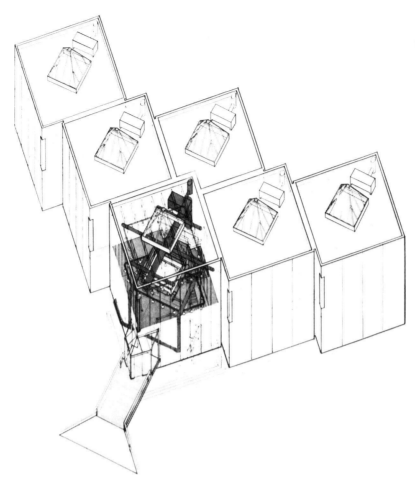

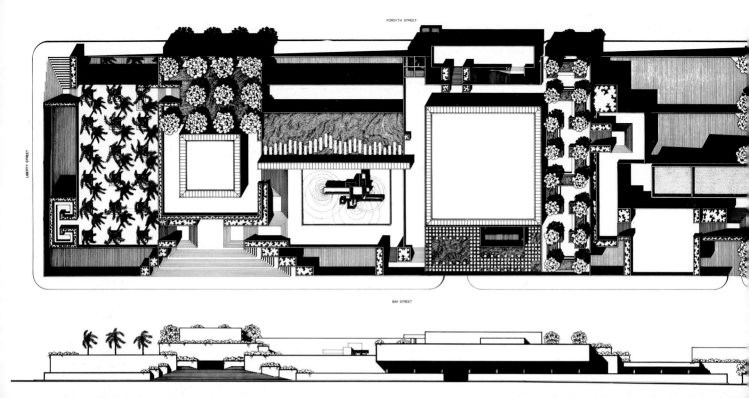

FORSYTH STREET

LIBERTY STREET

BAY STREET

Police Memorial

There is a strong coordination of the original presentation material in this project, which highlights the strong geometry and major visual features of the design. The combination of coordinated orthographic drawings and model photography taken from similar orientations helps to clarify the design. Even the rough study model below is indicative of the actual space, as demonstrated by the view of the completed building shown opposite.

Copley Place

Once this major retail mall was completed and occupied, photographs were taken from angles similar to those of the original presentation model. As in most projects, certain design changes and refinements were made. However, the major elements can be compared quite favorably. The photographs of the completed building were taken with a camera and lens combination similar to the camera used to shoot the model.

The method used here was to have a set of the original model slides in hand and to frame similar views in the camera viewfinder.

Performing Arts Center

This educational arts building complex was organized in a linear fashion to facilitate future expansion. The functions of art, music, and drama were grouped along an active circulation spine. This "street" gives identity to the complex and provides a visual and physical link for the three departments. The traditional simple forms of presentation depicted the original design scheme through rendered elevations and model photography. The final project expresses the character invoked in the original sketches.

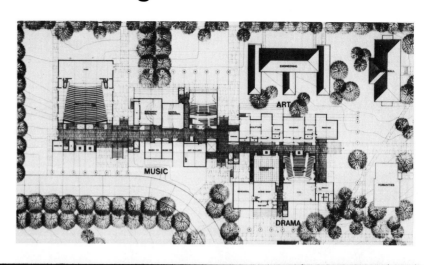

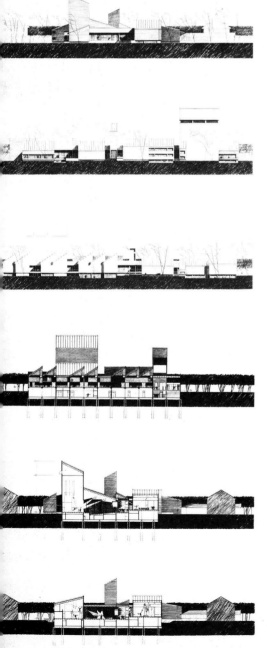

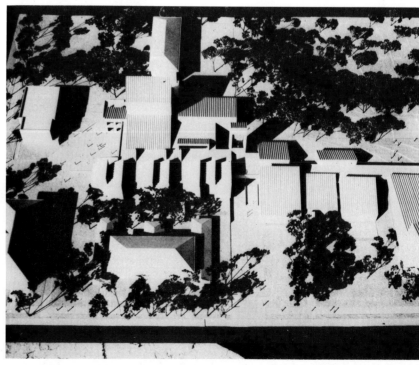

Cutler Ridge Showroom

The early sketches for this project clearly define the conceptual thinking behind its execution. The front facade of the masonry structure is fractured, then pulled apart into three main elements. The profile of each segment that is pulled out fits exactly the void behind it. The concept is clearly shown in the model photo taken from an aerial viewpoint. The photo of the finished building also highlights the concept very clearly.

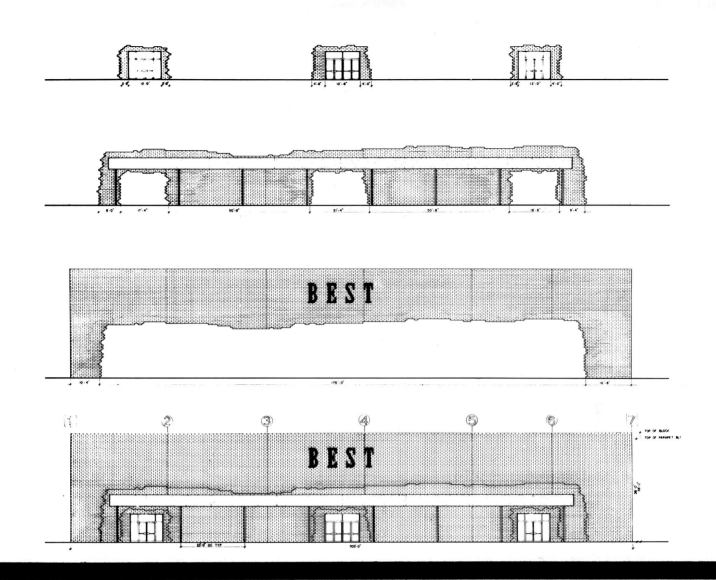

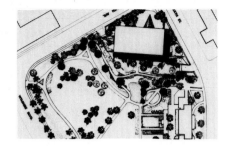

CNA Park Place

The original model used for design study and presentation on this office project was photographed out of doors to catch reflections from clouds in the sky. A similar model photo was superimposed into a photo of the actual site with similar clouds in the sky (below) for a more realistic appearance. This view is more convincing and closer to the actual completed project.

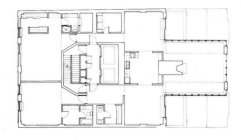

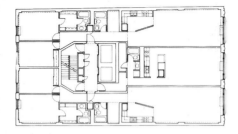

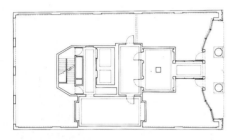

Apartment Tower

This structure continues the monumental quality that has been a tradition of building in the area in which it is located. Early presentation sketches concentrated on the design of the entryway and top of the building. The upper stories step back for terraced penthouse apartments. The side walls were ornamented with color panels since windows were precluded on the lot line.

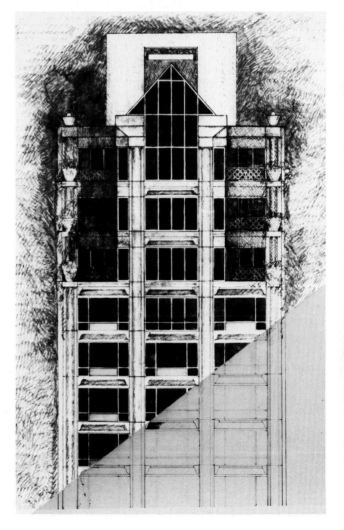

Multi-cat Research Tower

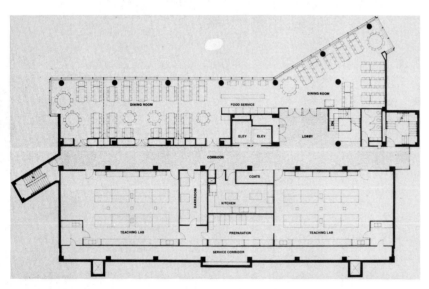

This multicategorical (multi-cat) research tower is a facility for the College of Veterinary Medicine. The 11-story building houses laboratories and office space. The interior organization is expressed by the two contrasting elevations. The office and classrooms have a glass facade while the laboratory side is all brick. The complex ventilation system utilizes three air intake "snorkles" which draw in fresh air. The used air is exhausted on the opposite side through the high multiple "nostrils." The original model photographs, taken from each side, express the same character as the completed project.

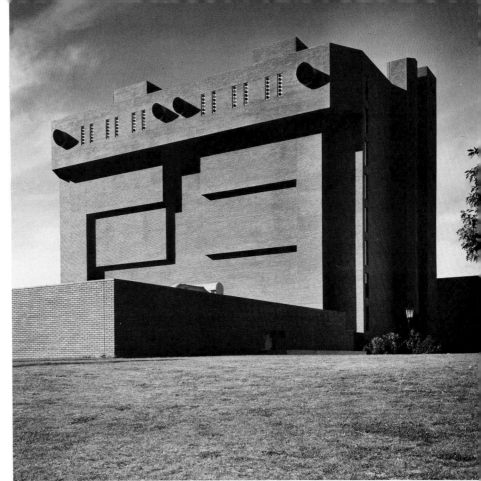
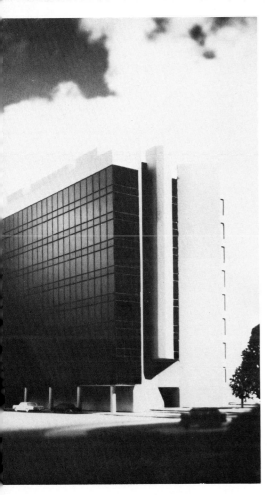

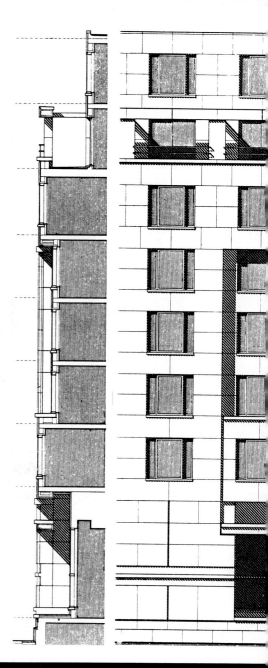

One Logan Square

This completed structure resembles the original presentation material very closely. A large-scale drawing of the lower part of the structure is shown in comparison to the actual site. A cutaway section explains the geometry of the facade and window treatment.

Hercules

This project is shown in two versions that are somewhat indistinguishable without clues. The view on the left is a photomontage of the model set into the site, and the one on the far right is a view of the completed project.

Design
Credits

3 4 5 6 7 8 9 10 11 12 13 14 15

31 32 33 34 35 36 37 38 39 40 41 42 43

59 60 61 62 63 64 65 66 67 68 69 70 71

87 88 89 90 91 92 93 94 95 96 97 98 99

115 116 117 118 119 120 121 122 123 124 125 126 127

143 144 145 146 147 148 149 150 151 152 153 154 155

171 172 173 174 175 176 177 178 179 180 181 182 183

199 200 201 202 203 204 205 206 207 208 209 210 211

227 228 229 230 231 232 233

223

DESIGN SIMULATION
Computer generated images
By SKOK Systems Incorporated.

II-III

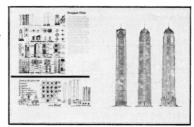

DESIGN STUDIES
BANK OF SOUTHWEST
TOWER
Houston, Texas
Murphy/Jahn
Chicago, Illinois

12-13

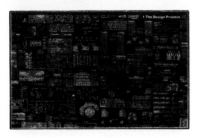

THE DESIGN PROCESS
PRESENTATION PLANNING
Prof. Edward T. White, A.I.A.
Florida Agricultural &
Mechanical University,
Tallahassee, Florida

VIII-I

DRAWING SIMULATION
PACIFIC LUTHERAN
UNIVERSITY MUSIC CENTER
Tacoma, Washington
Perkins & Will
Chicago, Illinois
Design and drawings by
Ralph Johnson
Model photography:
Orlando R. Cabanban

14-15

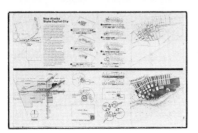

PROGRAMMING
BRANCH CAMPUS FOR
COCHISE COLLEGE
Architecture One, Ltd.
Tucson, Arizona

2-3

PRIX-de-ROME
Drawings of classical Greek
architecture from the Ecole
des BeauxArts, from an
exhibition at the IBM Gallery
of Art and Science, New York
City.

16-17

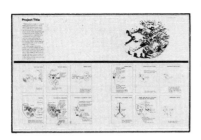

ORIENTATION
DESIGN ANALYSIS - HALL
MERCER HOSPITAL
Perry, Dean, Rogers & Partners:
Architects, Inc.
Boston, Massachusetts

4-5

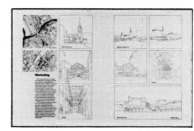

THEATER DISTRICT
Beckley/Myers, Architects
Milwaukee, Wisconsin
Delineator: Steven Greiczek

18-19

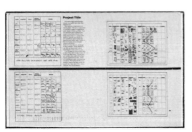

METHODOLOGY
Perry, Dean, Rogers & Partners:
Architects, Inc.
Boston, Massachusetts

6-7

GATEWAY PLAZA
GATEWAY PLAZA IN
WINSTON-SALEM, NORTH
CAROLINA
Designers: Archipelagos
Architects: Merrill Pasco, Ferd
Johns
Developer: Charles E. Fraser
Associates, Inc.

20-21

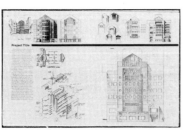

DESIGN PROCESS
INSTITUTE FOR ADVANCED
BIOMEDICAL RESEARCH,
OREGON HEALTH SCIENCES
UNIVERSITY
Zimmer Gunsul Frasca
Partnership
Portland, Oregon

8-9

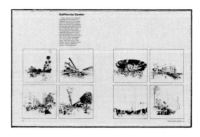

CALIFORNIA CENTER
Bunker Hill Competition
Los Angeles, California
Architects: Arthur Erickson
Associates; Kaminitzer Cotton
Vreeland; Gruen Associates
Drawings by Robert McIlhargey

22-23

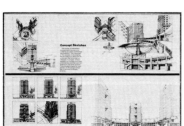

CONCEPT SKETCHES
PLAZA ONE
Dewberry & Davis
Fairfax, Virginia
Drawings by A.E. Cromer

10-11

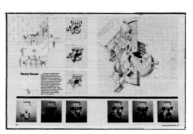

HEALY HOUSE
Estero, Florida
Brian Healy, Architect
Brooklyn, New York

24-25

224

KIVA SPORTS CENTER
Beaver Creek, Colorado
Sandy & Babcock
San Francisco, California
Delineator:
Carlos Deniz Associates

26-27

PENNINGTON BIOMEDICAL CENTER
John Desmond and Associates
Baton Rouge, Louisiana
Delineator: John Desmond

40-41

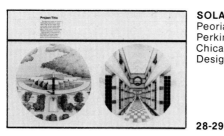

SOLAR-RAY
Peoria, Illinois
Perkins & Will
Chicago, Illinois
Design by Ralph Johnson

28-29

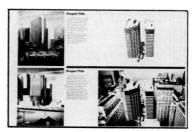

175 WATER STREET
LOWER BROADWAY
Fox & Fowle Architects, P.C.
New York, New York
Photography: Louis Checkman
Rendering by Tesla

42-43

PHILLIPS PETROLEUM
HEADQUARTERS,
Bartlesville, Oklahoma
Hellmuth, Obata & Kassabaum
Inc., St. Louis, Missouri
Delineator: Robert Watel, Jr.

30-31

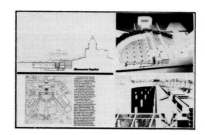

MINNESOTA CAPITOL
Steven Holl & James Tanner,
Architects
New York, New York

44-45

PHILLIPS POINT
West Palm Beach, Florida
Hellmuth, Obata & Kassabaum
Inc., St. Louis, Missouri
Delineators: Robert Watel, Jr.,
and Stephen W. Parker

32-33

MINNESOTA CAPITOL
2nd PLACE WINNER
Dellinger/Lee Associates
Charlotte, North Carolina
Photography:
Gordon Schenck Associates

46-47

KELLOGG'S
Hellmuth, Obata & Kassabaum
Inc., St. Louis, Missouri
Delineators: Robert Watel Jr.,
and Stephen W. Parker

34-35

MINNESOTA CAPITOL
(See credits under Pg. 46-47.)

48-49

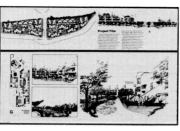

HOUSING PROJECT
Vallejo, California
Sandy & Babcock
San Francisco, California
Delineator: Mark Pechenik

36-37

HORIZON HILL CENTER
Arquitectonica
Coral Gables, Florida
Delineator: Orest

THE ATLANTIS
Arquitectonica
Coral Gables, Florida
Delineator: Orest

50-51

MIAMI HOTEL
OCEAN CLUB
Miami Beach, Florida
Perkins & Will
Chicago, Illinois
Design by Ralph Johnson

38-39

COPLEY PLACE
The Architects Collaborative
Cambridge, Massachusetts
Drawings by Howard Associates

52-53

Design Credits 225

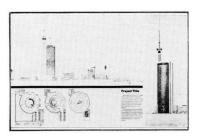

HUMANA
Humana Inc,
Louisville, Kentucky
Foster Associates
London U.K.

54-55

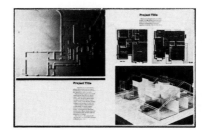

BRAILLE HOUSE
Moore Grover Harper, PC
Essex, Connecticut
Tactile blueprint:
William H. Grover, A.I.A.

TRANSPARENT MODEL
American Art
Downey, California

68-69

VANCOUVER TRANSIT
Allen Parker & Associates
Architects & Planners
Vancouver, B.C.
Thompson Berurch Pratt
Architects & Planners
Vancouver, B.C.
Delineator: Ron Love

56-57

BONN COMPETITION
West Germany
Director of Design: Professor
Otto Piene, Cambridge
Architects: Hans-Christian
Lischewski, Peter Droege
Model builder: William Schafer
Model photography:
Hans-Christian Lischewski

70-71

VANCOUVER TRANSIT

(See credits under Pg. 56-57.)

58-59

LYDELL SQUARE
RESEARCH PROJECT
Project Director: Professor
Antero Markelin, University of
Stuttgart, West Germany
Model builder: Bernd Fahle,
Hans-Christian Lischewski
Photography:
Hans-Christian Lischewski
Equipment: Storz, Weinberger
72-73

EXPO 86
Bruno Freschi, Architect
Drawing Team:
Robert McIlhargey
Lori Brown
Eugene Radvenis
Jim Hancock
Sherry Hancock
Computer Isometric:
'H.A. Simons (International) Ltd.
60-61

LYDELL SQUARE

(See credits under Pg. 72-73.)

74-75

EXPO 86
Waisman Dewar Groot
Architects and Planners
Drawings by: Robert
McIlhargey and Lori Brown

62-63

MODEL SIMULATORS
RESEARCH PROJECT
Project Director: Professor
Antero Markelin, University of
Stuttgart, West Germany
Model simulators: University
of Lund, Sweden
Photography: Hans-Christian
Lischewski

76-77

B.C. PLACE
Dave Podmore, Dir. Planning
Peter Busby, Design Architect
Arthur Erickson Associates
Vancouver, B.C.
Fisher Friedman
San Francisco, California
Drawings by Robert
McIlhargey, Lori Brown, and
Eugene Radvenis
64-65

MODEL SIMULATORS
RESEARCH PROJECT
Project Director: Professor
Antero Markelin, University of
Stuttgart, West Germany
Model simulators:
University of Delft, Holland
University of Wageningen,
Holland

78-79

MODEL SIMULATION
COPLEY PLACE
TAC, The Architects
Collaborative, Inc.
Cambridge, Massachusetts
Model photography: Most Media

66-67

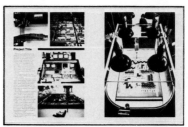

MODEL SIMULATORS
Professor Antero Markelin,
University of Stuttgart, West
Germany
Model simulators: Eindhoven,
Holland
Institute of Urban & Regional
Development
U.C., Berkeley, California
Photography:
Peter Boesselmann   **80-81**

ARTS & MEDIA FACILITIES
I.M. Pei and Partners, New York
Model photography:
Hans-Christian Lischewski,
Scott Fisher, Kristina Hooper
Facility used: The Architecture
Machine Group, M.I.T.

82-83

ENGINEERING MODELS
USA Models
Colwyn, Pennsylvania

96-97

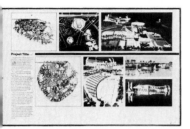

UNIVERSITY OF BAGHDAD STADIUM
TAC, The Architects
Collaborative, Inc.
Cambridge, Massachusetts
Peter W. Morton, AIA, Architect
Model photography: Most Media

84-85

PLANT MODEL PHOTOGRAPHY
Model photography: Most Media
98-99

UNIVERSITY OF BAGHDAD LIBRARY
TAC, The Architects
Collaborative, Inc.
Cambridge, Massachusetts
Peter W. Morton, AIA, Architect
Model photography: Most Media

86-87

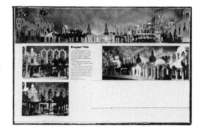

WONDERWALL
1984 LOUISIANA WORLD
EXPOSITION
Perez Associates
Studio 2/Architects
New Orleans, Louisiana
Design: Leonard Salvato and
Arthur Anderson
Consultants: Charles Moore and
William Turnbull
Model: Ray Knishito
Model photography:
Alan Karchmer   **100-101**

UNIVERSITY OF BAGHDAD HOUSING
TAC, The Architects
Collaborative, Inc.
Cambridge, Massachusetts
Peter W. Morton, AIA, Architect
Model photography: Most Media

88-89

PHASED DEVELOPMENT
FIRST UNITED METHODIST
Seattle, Washington
STEPHAN SQUARE
Calgary, Canada
Skidmore, Owings & Merrill
Portland, Oregon
Photography: Ranson & Nodwell

102-103

UNIVERSITY OF BAGHDAD ADMINISTRATION BUILDING
TAC, The Architects
Collaborative, Inc.
Cambridge, Massachusetts
Model photography: Most Media

90-91

PHOTOMONTAGES
212 Stockton Street,
580 California Street
San Francisco, California
Square One Film & Video
San Francisco, California
Photography:
Hartmut H. Gerdes, AICP

104-105

SCIENCE FOUNDATION
FOUNDATION FOR THE
ADVANCEMENT OF SCIENCE
Kuwait
TAC, The Architects
Collaborative, Inc.
Cambridge, Massachusetts
Alex Cvijanovic, AIA, Architect
Model photography: Most Media

92-93

PARK AVENUE SYNAGOGUE
Conklin Rossant
New York, New York
Model Photography:
Louis Checkman

106-107

ENGINEERING MODELS
American Engineering Model
Society (AEMS)
Aiken, South Carolina

94-95

LINCOLN WEST
New York, New York
Socma Corporation
New York, New York
Rafael Vinoly, Architects, P.C.

108-109

Design Credits 227

TEHRAN INT'L AIRPORT
TAMS - Engineers, Architects &
Planners, New York, New York
Design by Prokosch, Pierce,
Zdzienicki, Naples
Model photography:
Jack Horner
Drawing by Gregory Ihnatowicz

110-111

PANORAMA PHOTOGRAPHY
BOSTON CITY HALL PLAZA
Photography: Hans-Christian
Lischewski, Martha Leinroth
Graphics: Hans-Christian
Lischewski

124-125

OMNI
NORFOLK GARDENS
Osment Models, Inc.
Linn Creek, Missouri

112-113

NORTH RIVER
WATER POLUTION
CONTROL PLANT
TAMS Engineers, Architects &
Planners
New York, New York
Design by C. Theodore Long

126-127

PEACHTREE SUMMIT
MERCANTILE CENTER
Osment Models, Inc.
Linn Creek, Missouri

114-115

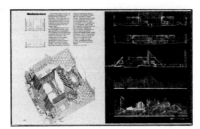

MEDIATECTURE
A HOUSE FOR KARL
FRIEDRICH SCHINKEL
Architects: Hans-Christian
Lischewski, Paul Johnson

128-129

COPLEY PLACE
TAC, The Architects
Collaborative
Cambridge, Massachusetts
Model photography: Most Media
Photography: William Schaefer
116-117

MEDIATECTURE

(See credits under Pg. 128-129.

HOLOGRAM
Model for the Parc des Folies a la
Villette; commissioned by the
Musee National des Sciences
Techniques et de l'Industrie,
Paris, France
Hologram by Francois Mazzero
and Jean-Francois Moreau of
Departement Ap-holographie,
DEMIN (Paris, France)
Collection of Museum of
Holography, New York City
Photography: Ronald R. Erickson
118-119

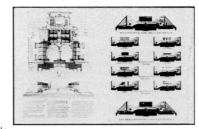

130-131

**NORMAN SPIVOCK
RESIDENCE**
Donald Clever Inc., Design
San Francisco, California

120-121

3-D VISUALIZATION
3-IMAGE LENTICULAR
PHOTOGRAPHY OF THE ART
AND MEDIA TECHNOLOGY
BUILDING, M.I.T.
I.M. Pei and Partners, New York
Lenticular image: Scott Fisher
Hologram: Donald Thornton
Model and insert photography:
Hans-Christian Lischewski
132-133

FOUNTAIN PLACE
Photo-Synthesis Inc.
Dallas, Texas

134-135

3-D MODEL VISUALIZATION
Stereo Images and Stereo
Photography: Hans Christian
Lischewski

122-123

FUJIYA SIGN
Donald Clever Inc., Design
San Francisco, California

136-137

COMPUTER GRAPHICS
ARTS & MEDIA FACILITIES
Cambridge
Computer graphics applications:
Hans-Christian Lischewski
Facility used: Architecture
Machine Group, M.I.T.

138-139

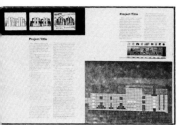

COMPUTER SKETCHES
Project Director:
Hans-Christian Lischewski
Facility used: Architecture
Machine Group, M.I.T.
Design modifications done by
Hans-Christian Lischewski

140-141

ALAMO SQUARE
RESEARCH PROJECT
Project Director: Hans-
Christian Lischewski,
Programmers: Daniel
Franzblau, Walter Bender, Paul
Heckbert
Facility used: Architecture
Machine Group, M.I.T.
Renderings: Hans-Christian
Lischewski   **142-143**

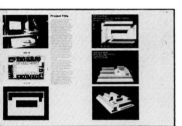

"N" PLAN
RESEARCH PROJECT
Project Director: Hans-Christian
Lischewski
Programmers: Daniel
Franzblau, Walter Bender, Mark
Vershel
Facility used: Architecture
Machine Group, M.I.T.

144-145

COMPUTER WALL PAINTING
Project Director:
Hans-Christian Lischewski
Programmers:
Daniel Franzblau, Walter Bender,
Mark Vershel
Facility used: Architecture
Machine Group, M.I.T.
Computer graphics plotter by:
Professor Ron McNeill, Visible
Language Workshop, M.I.T.
146-147

PAINTER HILL HOUSE
Redroof Design, New York
Renderings: Peter Cohen,
Hans-Christian Lischewski,
Yann Weymouth,
Daniel Franzblau
Facility used: Architecture
Machine Group, M.I.T.

148-149

**3-D COMPUTER
VISUALIZATION**
Computer generated images by
SKOK Systems Incroporated

150-151

VANDERBILT HOSPITAL
Russo & Sonder
New York, New York
Computer graphics:
Bonnie Biaforie,
Hans-Christian Lischewski

152-153

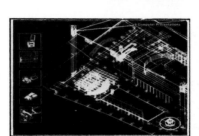

GATEWAY PLAZA
Interactive Graphics Services
Company Inc.,
Indianapolis, Indiana
Computer images and
Photography: Charlie Chappelle
Designers: Archipelagos
Architects: Merrill Pasco,
Ferd Johns

154-155

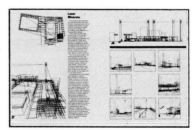

3-PHASE MASSING STUDY
Everett I. Brown Company
Indianapolis, Indiana

156-157

COMPUTER PRESENTATIONS
PERFORMING ARTS CENTER
Milwaukee, Wisconsin
Design Professionals, Inc.
Jerry Rubin, A.I.A., I.B.D.
Harry J. Wirth, A.I.A., ED, I.B.D.
Kenneth Cheng, I.B.D.
Computers: Milwaukee Area
Technical College,
Computervision Corp.
158-159

COMPUTER PRESENTATIONS

(See credits under Pg. 158-159.)

160-161

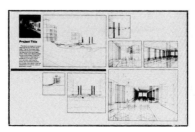

COMPUTER PRESENTATIONS

(See credits under Pg. 158-159.)

162-163

MT. WASHINGTON CAMPUS
UNITED STATES FIDELITY
AND GUARANTY COMPANY
BUILDING
RTKL Associates, Inc.
Baltimore, Maryland
Model photography:
David Whitcomb

164-165

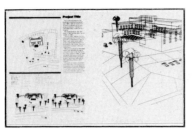

HOSPITAL PROJECT
Graphic Horizons, Inc.
Boston, Massachusetts
Design by: The Stewart Design
Group, Boston

166-167

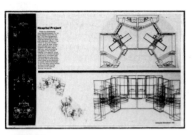

HOSPITAL PROJECT

(See credits under Pg. 166-167.)

168-169

SPACE MODELING
Construction Systems
Associates, Inc.
Amadeus M. Burger
Marietta, Georgia

170-171

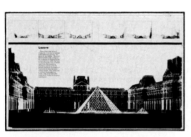

LOUVRE
I.M. Pei and Partners, New York
Otto Buchholz
Coordinator: Steve Oles
Computer images:
Computervision Corp.

172-173

B.C. PLACE
Computer drawings by:
H.A. Simons (International) Ltd.
Vancouver, B.C.

174-175

B.C. PLACE
SOUTH SLOPES RESIDEN-
TIAL NEIGHBORHOOD
H.A. Simons (International) Ltd.
Vancouver, B.C.
Drawing and photomontage:
Robert McIlhargey

176-177

SEQUENTIAL SIMULATION
DARPA RESEARCH PROJECT
MDA-903-78-C-0039
Surrogate travel user:
Hans-Christian Lischewski

178-179

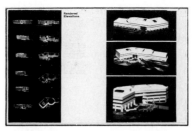

FARM CREDIT BANK
Everett I. Brown Company
Indianapolis, Indiana

180-181

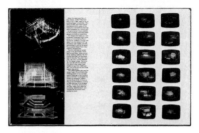

WOLF TRAP
FILENE CENTER FOR THE
PERFORMING ARTS
Dewberry & Davis, Architect
and Engineers, Fairfax, Virginia
Video presentation: Intergraph

182-183

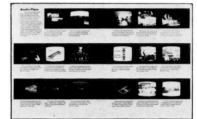

NABISCO
NABISCO TECHNOLOGY
CENTER
Haines Lundberg Waehler, AEI
New York, New York

184-185

FIRST CENTER
Southfield, Michigan
Harley Ellington Pierce & Yee
Architects
Video by Ken Paul Associates,
Detroit, Michigan

186-187

F.D.R. MEMORIAL
Lawrence Halprin and Associates
Film by Glen Fleck

188-189

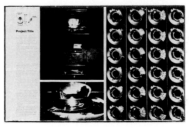

**ASPEN PROJECT: VIDEODISC
SIMULATION**
DARPA RESEARCH PROJECT
MDA-903-78-C-0039
Surrogate Travel
Principal Investigator:
Professor Nicholas
Negroponte, M.I.T., Cambridge,
Massachusetts
Program Director: Professor
Andrew Lippman
Production: Dr. Richard Bolt,
John Borden, Steven Gregory,
Kristina Hooper, Professor
Richard Leacock, Hans-
Christian Lischewski, Michael
Naimark, Becky Allen, Walter
Bender, Scott Fisher, Bernd
Kracke, Ann Marion, Robert
Mohl, Bill Parker, Marek
Zalewski

190-191
192-193

230

ASPEN PROJECT: VIDEODISC SIMULATION

(See credits under Pg. 190-193.)

194-195

COPLEY PLACE
TAC, The Architects
Collaborative, Inc.
Cambridge, Massachusetts
Howard F. Elkus, FAIA,
Architect
Model photography: Most Media
Photography: William Schaefer

208-209

ASPEN PROJECT: VIDEODISC SIMULATION

(See credits under Pg. 190-193.)

196-197

PERFORMING ARTS CENTER
University of Minnesota, Morris
Ralph Rapson & Associates, Inc.
Minneapolis, Minnesota

210-211

COMPLETED PROJECTS
JACKSON COUNTY
MEMORIAL HOSPITAL,
Altus, Oklahoma
Kirkham Michael & Associates
Omaha, Nebraska
Drawings by: Jim Hohenstein
Photography: Joy Arnold

198-199

CUTLER RIDGE SHOWROOM
Design, drawings, model, and
photography by SITE Projects
Inc.

212-213

ALTUS HOSPITAL
JACKSON COUNTY
MEMORIAL HOSPITAL

(See credits under Pg. 198-199.)

200-201

CNA PARK PLACE
Langdon Wilson Mumper
Architects
Los Angeles, California
Photography:
Wayne Thom Photography

214-215

CHARLES CENTER TOWERS
Conklin Rossant
New York, New York
Photography: Louis Checkman

202-203

APARTMENT TOWER
320 NORTH MICHIGAN AVE.
Booth/Hansen & Associates,
Ltd., Chicago, Illinois
Photography: Timothy Hursely

216-217

ART GALLERY
JOAN WHITNEY PAYSON
GALLERY OF ART
Westbrook College
Portland, Maine
TAC, The Architects
Collaborative, Inc.,
Cambridge, Massachusetts
Photography: Nick Wheeler

204-205

MULTI-CAT
MULTICATEGORICAL
RESEARCH TOWER
Cornell University
Ulrich Franzen & Associates
New York, New York
Photography:
Norman McGrath **218-219**

POLICE MEMORIAL
William Morgan Architects
Jacksonville, Florida
Photography: Otto Baitz

206-207

ONE LOGAN SQUARE
Philadelphia, Pa.
Kohn Pedersen Fox Associates
PC, New York, New York
Photomontage: Jack Horner
Photography: Norman McGrath
Drawing: Andrea Simitch

HERCULES
Wilmington, Delaware
Photomontage: Jack Horner
Photography: John Pottle
220-221

Index